THE DOBERMANN

POPULAR DOGS' BREED SERIES

THE DOBERMANN

FRED CURNOW

AND

JEAN FAULKS

POPULAR DOGS

London Melbourne Sydney Auckland Johannesburg

Popular Dogs Publishing Co. Ltd

An imprint of the Hutchinson Publishing Group

3 Fitzroy Square, London w i p 6 j d

Hutchinson Group (Australia) Pty Ltd
30–32 Cremorne Street, Richmond South, Victoria 3121
PO Box 151, Broadway, New South Wales 2007

Hutchinson Group (NZ) Ltd
32–34 View Road, PO Box 40–086, Glenfield, Auckland 10

Hutchinson Group (SA) (Pty) Ltd
PO Box 337, Bergvlei 2012, South Africa

First published 1972
Second edition, revised, 1975
Third edition, revised, 1976
Fourth edition, revised, 1979
Fifth edition, revised, 1980
© Fred Curnow and Jean Faulks 1972, 1975, 1976, 1979 and 1980

Printed in Great Britain at The Anchor Press Ltd
and bound by Wm Brendon & Son Ltd
both of Tiptree, Essex

ISBN 0 09 143140 9

To Julia Curnow
without whose devotion to the Dobermann
this book would never have been written

CONTENTS

ILLUSTRATIONS

Training for manwork

Ch. Tavey's Stormy Acacia
Bred by Mrs. J. Curnow
Owned by Mrs. E. Gladstone

Training with the dumb-bell

Mr. J. Carpenter with his guide-dog

Trudi of Ely demonstrates a soft mouth
Bred by Mrs. C. Dunsford
Owned by Mr. A. Hopkin

Dollar Premium, T.D.ex, W.D.ex, U.D.ex, C.D.ex
Bred by Mrs. E. Peckham
Owned by Mrs. C. Hooper

Ch. Royaltains Babette of Tavey
Bred by Mrs. J. Curnow
Owned by Mrs. P. Gledhill and Miss P. Quinn

Arawak Perfecta
Bred by Mr. and Mrs. Robert Abel
Owned by Mrs. J. Curnow

IN THE TEXT

Author's Introduction

It goes without saying that unless you have a love and admiration for dogs it is pointless to own one or, worse still, more than one. A thoroughbred dog is no longer a status symbol; it is demanding on your time and patience and needs a great deal of care. If you have a natural affection for the canine species and require a companion who will return fidelity for love there is no reason at all why a Dobermann should not be considered.

Should you be devoid of kindness and patience it is better to give up all idea of owning or being owned by a dog, because these feelings between dog and man are reciprocal. A natural love of dogs will make the ownership considerably more pleasurable than if you buy one simply as a talking point in the local pub, especially when it comes to lead and house training, etc., which is an essential part of the partnership.

It is for these reasons that Jean Faulks and I have spent a couple of years thinking about and eventually writing this book and I hope that the chapters contained herein will help newcomers and experts alike more fully to appreciate dogs in general, and Dobermanns in particular.

It is imperative that you have a good knowledge of feeding, exercising and rearing, an idea of how the Dobermann was evolved, and if you have a knowledge of how it has fared in different countries the information should make the possession of this lovely breed all the more enjoyable. The original Dobermann was quite a different animal from the powerful, elegant dog we see these days, and it is up to you, should breeding be contemplated, to make sure that you help the breed to progress and reach an even higher standard instead of allowing it to deteriorate.

When writing this book Jean Faulks and I have tried to cover all aspects of the breed, she handling the working side and I the development of Dobermanns from early days. In addition, chapters have been included that could be of assistance to both newcomers and exhibitors. It is hoped that readers will learn about conformation, choosing and rearing a puppy, training and general care of this wonderful breed.

Incidentally, the Dobermann, with its clean, noble and elegant line, is today one of the most beautiful animals in the world and while I have concentrated on what is termed the beauty aspect it should not be forgotten that the Dobermann was first evolved as a guard and working dog. Jean has dealt most fully with this characteristic and but for her help in this direction, *The Dobermann* would have been incomplete.

Obviously, a dog that is a show specimen, and with a temperament that makes it an excellent guard, is the ideal companion. There are many Dobermanns in Britain, Europe and the U.S.A. that compete successfuly in the breed, obedience and working events, and it must indeed be a pleasure to own such a specimen. In other words, although the Dobermann was originally evolved as a dog with the utmost intelligence, capable of working all day long, he must also be an aristocratic, elegant, noble and beautifully proportioned animal.

In my opinion the Americans have reached nearer the ideal than any other nation in this respect and it is pleasing to see that while several years ago they were producing rather large specimens, by far the majority these days are of the correct height according to both American and British standards.

In Germany, the original home of the breed, Dobermanns are approximately of the same size as those in Britain, and having seen some of the top exhibits at the Berlin, Düsseldorf, Dortmund and Wiesbaden shows I am convinced that we in Britain have exhibits in both quality and quantity superior to those in Germany. This condition did not exist until a few years ago, prior to which we were some way behind the Germans in overall quality. Having in mind that the breed was practically unknown in Britain until 1947, we can be very proud of the fact that specimens now produced in these isles can compete with those bred in Scandinavia, Holland, Portugal, Belgium, France, Switzerland and Germany.

I am indebted to George Tunnicliff who drew the several

sketches which are essential to illustrate certain points and I do most sincerely express my gratitude for this invaluable assistance. Further, I would like to thank Len Charles, my partner, for his help in compiling the chapter on feeding, his knowledge on this subject being superior to most others.

Len Carey, of the U.S.A., once proud owner and exhibitor of the late Am. Ch. Rancho Dobe's Storm, probably the most successful Dobermann ever to be exhibited, is also to be thanked for his encouragement and suggestions which have enabled me to explain more fully the various parts in the Standard of the breed.

Joanna Walker of the U.S.A. and Inge Dallman of Germany have also greatly helped with research on Dobermanns in the United States and in Europe and many others have quite unwittingly helped in various ways, especially those with whom I have discussed the breed and from whom much has been learned and with whom many sincere friendships have been cemented and enjoyed.

As I have already said, this book would have been incomplete without the four chapters (8 to 11) dealing with obedience, working trials, working tests and police service—and I must express my indebtedness to Jean Faulks for having contributed these interesting and educational sections. Jean, in my opinion, is one of the most dedicated and certainly one of the most able amateur trainers of Dobermanns in Great Britain and her chapters have brought out the high qualities of our breed in a manner no other writer could have done.

I am confident that you will, as I did, enjoy reading about the inherent intelligence and ability that every good Dobermann should, if correctly trained, be able to demonstrate. I personally have no penchant for training dogs in obedience competition or working tests, but I have learned from my experiences in the show ring and by having Dobermanns around me in my own home that one can never bring a dog's intelligence up to the level of that enjoyed by human beings. It is essential that this be fully recognised and an attempt made to meet the dog halfway by raising his understanding to some degree, using his natural bent as a mimic and his ability to absorb everything repetitive, while at the same time employing a little doggy psychology. Hard, brutal methods will get you nowhere because the love and affection a dog is prepared to give an owner he respects will be destroyed unless there is mutual trust and companionship. A dog is not a machine and is capable of giving devotion that no other animal can emulate, so it is up to you to treat him as you would a friendly pupil until such time as you both consider yourselves equals.

The chapter Jean has written on the Dobermann in working trials and the appendices she has compiled are the result of intense research over a long time and as they cover a period of more than twenty years they will, I am sure, from now on be of great value as reference material on what has transpired in working trials, particularly in relation to Dobermanns, over that period.

1972   F.C.

In this second edition, Jean Faulks and I have made a few minor revisions to the text. We have also brought the appendices up-to-date.

1974   F.C.

For the third edition, in which two additional photographs have been included, we have again made some small revisions to our text and brought the appendices up-to-date once more.

1976   F.C.

A few more minor corrections – mainly to bring prices up-to-date – have been made to this fourth edition, and we have again extended the appendices.

After twenty-five-years as a Dobermann owner and handler, with experience in every type of competition, Jean Faulks has now been approved by the Kennel Club to award Challenge Certificates in breed competition, working trials and obedience tests. She is only the second person in Great Britain to achieve this distinction, and the first ever connected with Dobermanns. I, for my part, who have written chapters 1–7, have judged the breed in many countries all over the world.

1979   F.C.

As Fred Curnow was in hospital at the time the fifth edition was called for, I have been asked by the publishers to bring up to date his part of this book as well as my own. I have therefore amended some prices given in chapter 5, updated Appendices A and B, and extended Appendix E in addition to those which are usually my responsibility.

1980   J.F.

Origin and Development of the Breed

THE history of the Dobermann, although veiled in mystery, is nevertheless intriguing and fascinating: intriguing because delving into any historical subject, and in particular when dealing with a specific breed of dog, arouses curiosity; fascinating because in tracing the ancestry of a dog the results can be educational and enable correct breeding programmes to be planned.

Many writers have tried to trace the origin of the Dobermann, but as no definite records were kept by the man who evolved this attractive and alert dog, most of what has been written is based on assumption; intelligent assumption, certainly, because due to the colour and conformation of the present-day Dobermann it is reasonable to assume that several breeds, each quite different from the others, were used in its evolution. I suppose that almost all breeds of dogs as we know them today were evolved by accident from a mixture of several types, but what I find fascinating is that although the Dobermann is a relatively new breed no detailed records of how it evolved are easily available.

What we do know, however, is that Louis Dobermann did not produce the breed by accident but used planned methods to arrive at the end result. Louis Dobermann of Apolda in the state of Thuringia, Germany, was a tax or rent collector during the 1880s and, being a dog lover, albeit one who liked aggressive animals, he decided to breed a dog that would be of help and protection to him when making his rounds. He had the added advantage of being the keeper of the dog pound into which all strays within his area were kept.

One can imagine the many cross-breeds, mongrels and pure-bred dogs that eventually found their way into Herr Dobermann's dog pound and the serious thought he must have given before selecting the several breeds necessary towards producing his ideal guard dog. Doubtless he had in mind a dog of average build so that it would scare off intruders and act as a positive guard. He also probably preferred a dog with a smooth, short coat to reduce unnecessary grooming, and, above all, he must have wanted stamina, intelligence and alertness so that his companion could travel with him during the many hours demanded by his work.

At that time there existed the German Pinscher, which was, according to photographs, a rather nondescript dog. However, this Pinscher had the reputation of being aggressive and alert and it was around that breed Louis Dobermann built his strain.

Even in those far-off days the Germans had developed the habit of cropping the ears of certain breeds and the Pinscher was among those who suffered this operation, the main purpose of which was to give a more alert and fearsome expression. Another reason for cropping was to reduce the size of pendulous ears, thus making it more difficult for other dogs to maintain a firm hold when fighting with those whose ears were almost non-existent. From the date of evolution of the breed and up to the early 1920s it was fashionable to crop ears to quite a small size, but more recently, in an attempt to add elegance and line to Dobermanns, Boxers, and Great Danes, both the Germans and the Americans have adopted what is known as 'the long crop'.

The Rottweiler, which readers will know is a massive, solid dog noted particularly for stamina and tracking power, was also introduced into the blood line and even today we occasionally see in some Dobermanns the slightly wavy coat inherited from the Rottweiler.

It is fact, however, that the Rottweiler did much to bring the Dobermann Pinscher into being and those enthusiasts who work their dogs should deeply appreciate Louis Dobermann's forethought when deciding to introduce the blood of such an intelligent dog into his blood lines. It is well perhaps at this stage to remind readers that while our breed is now known simply as the Dobermann, it was, up to 1957, known and registered in Britain as the Dobermann Pinscher. Kennel Club permission was given to drop the word Pinscher when it was pointed out that such nomenclature literally translated from the German meant Terrier, which type of dog the present-day Dobermann does not resemble in any way at all. Germany also eliminated the word Pinscher even before we in Britain took this step, but in America and several other countries the breed is still known by the double name.

It is generally accepted that the Manchester Terrier, which in those days was probably a larger dog than one sees in Britain these days, was also used in the evolution of the Dobermann, thus giving the short, shiny coat and the distinctive black-and-tan markings.

Undoubtedly the use of Manchester Terrier blood, besides adding colour and coat type to the present-day Dobermann, gave something towards the refinement, elegance and line, and even today we often see the distinctive black thumb markings which are typical of the Manchester breed on the toes of newly born Dobermanns. Fortunately, these dark markings on the toes as well as the white spots on the chest of young Dobermanns invariably disappear by the time the puppy is three to four months of age.

Some French enthusiasts of today consider that Beauceron blood was also introduced, thus accounting for size and colour. This is quite feasible because the Beauceron is also a solid, upstanding, bright and alert guard dog and the breed, or something very similar, was known to be in the district of Thuringia during the time Herr Dobermann was producing his own particular breed. Another reason for considering that the Beauceron was used in the evolution of the Dobermann is that this breed often carries a white patch on the chest which trait was very apparent in the original Dobermanns and still crops up occasionally today.

From my own studies of the Dobermann I am convinced that the Pointer, whether English or German type does not really matter, was also used when Louis Dobermann was slowly producing his ideal. Many a time when exercising my own dogs in adjacent woodland where birds and game can be found I have seen my dogs suddenly stop and point with the correct foreleg and tailset of a first-class Pointer. If we look back at some old photographs of the breed, a few of which can be found in Philipp

Gruenig's book on Dobermanns, we find a most extraordinary dog with a harsh coat standing about 22 inches at the shoulder. No doubt Louis Dobermann, although satisfied with the temperament he had bred into his dogs, was not exactly pleased with the lack of style every dog lover admires and it is reasonable to think, knowing the graceful and noble animal we see today, that some refinement was added by Louis Dobermann, or more probably by his successor Otto Goeller. This could easily have been the Greyhound, possibly black in colour, because of additional height, stamina and speed inherent in the dog.

What is really surprising is that Dobermanns of today breed so true to type and we must thank both Louis Dobermann and Otto Goeller, who continued his work, for being such highly selective and successful breeders. With no shadow of doubt it can be claimed, after studying photographs of Dobermanns from the 1900s up to the present day, that improvement in type has been tremendously progressive and I am confident that as time goes on, and if breeders will follow the example set by the two German originators who must have devoted much time to the subject, we can by selective breeding produce more and more dogs that tend towards the ideal. Of course, at the present time there are excellent dogs in almost every country in the world but there are also many more that do not fit correctly into the standard of the breed. It must surely be the wish of serious breeders to see more and more first-class Dobermanns being bred and exhibited and not just a large quantity of mediocre dogs walking our streets. Obviously it is preferable to own something of beauty that actually costs no more to buy and to keep than does something that does not evoke admiration when viewed by friends and the owner.

I have already mentioned Herr Goeller, also of Apolda, who was the man who took up the breed where Louis Dobermann left off. There is no doubt that the former gradually improved the overall quality of Dobermanns but even so, in 1899, when the breed was exhibited in Germany, one of the earliest critiques read:

'The Dobermann was still coarse throughout, his head showed heavy cheeks and the dogs had too wide and French fronts; in coats the dogs were too long and wavy, especially long on the neck and shanks. A lot of dogs were built too heavy, appearing more like a Rottweiler. This was the first show where Dobermanns entered in every class. The first Dobermanns were very sharp fellows with straw yellow markings, white spots on chest, sometimes appearing more grey in colour than black on account of their heavy undercoat. They did not make the impression of a uniform and well bred breed. However, exterior body deficiencies were made up by splendid qualities.'

Contrast the dogs described in that quotation with the uniform elegance of the Dobermanns one sees all over the world today. The fact that this dog has come so far and so quickly is not only a credit to the founders of the breed and those who succeeded them but also to the type of dog that has the inherent qualities of watchfulness and alertness, loyalty and fidelity to his family, aloofness to outsiders, his braininess, and his regard for property.

During the last year or two of the nineteenth century an improvement in quality was noticed and although by that time the Dobermann cult had spread into many parts of Germany it was in the state of Apolda, where the breed originated, that this evolution really took place. Exhibits with the names of Lux, Schnupp and Rambo drew much attention to themselves, and the first-named, mated to Tilly v. Groenland, produced a five-star litter. Otto Goeller mated Schnupp to a bitch registered as Helmtrude, and it was a grandson of these two, registered as Lord v. Ried, that has gone down in German history as a pillar of the breed.

At this time both black and brown Dobermanns were being born, but it was not until 1906 that the first blue dog appeared. It would seem that there was no objection to this new colour, so the standard was amended to make all three colours acceptable. Two years beforehand there appeared in Germany what has been described as one of the mightiest stud dogs of any age or breed. This dog, Hellegraf v. Thueringen, is further described as a paragon of beauty, perfection and power, but as this comment was made by an author as far back as 1939, the present-day Dobermanns could not have been taken into consideration.

And so we go on for a few more years, learning from photographs of a gradual improvement in quality, style and refinement until in 1906 Sturmfried v. Ilm Athen was born, scoring particularly in nobility and richness of colour. This dog had the reflected glory of having produced a grandson, Modern v. Ilm Athen, the blood of which is carried in almost every Dobermann in the world today. It is pointless to go through the evolution of the Dobermann year by year, but each brought out excellent, average, and mediocre specimens. Some were terribly aggressive and others were complete cowards; nevertheless careful breeding programmes adopted by the more responsible breeders in Germany helped to standardise type and further improve overall refinement as distinct from the cloddy animal of twenty years before.

However, this improvement was not confined to German-bred dogs because about this time several kennels in Switzerland and Holland had been established and were working to a systematic programme. It was in 1912 that the first Isabella-coloured Dobermann was born in Germany and I am sure that the oft repeated assertion that this fawn shade is the result of continued mixture of brown blood lines is correct. In the U.S.A. I have seen a couple of fawn Dobermanns which quite candidly do not appeal to my sense of good colour and, as a matter of fact, up to the time of publishing this book, Isabellas or fawns are not acceptable in the majority of countries throughout the world.

Incidentally, thinking about this colour termed 'Isabella', I have found out that there are several different stories about how this shade obtained its name. Some folk say that Isabella is the colour of old linen, basing their assumption on the tale of Queen Isabella of Spain, who, when her capital city was surrounded by enemies, swore that she would not change her linen until the siege was lifted. A period of three years elapsed before the enemy was dispersed and one can easily imagine that the Queen's linen was by that time the colour of parchment.

Another story regarding this colour is that Queen Isabella, who apparently was a most dominant personality, ordered that all Spain's royal horses should be of her favourite colour, which was a shade of yellow. As a result, all horses of that colour in Europe, much of which was under the influence of Spain in those far-off days, became known as Isabella horses, and apparently this term has persisted right up to the present day. Spanish adventurers sailing to America took many such specimens with them, some of which escaped into the plains and bred in the wild state. From these descended the Palamino, a colour now popular in many countries, so it is fair to assume that the term originally applied to horses may well apply to dogs. However, Isabella is not a precise term of colour and could equally range between parchment and fawn.

One of the best bitches ever to be born in Holland was Angola v. Grammont and when eventually she went to the White Gate Kennels of Philadelphia, U.S.A., she produced outstanding progeny. As I have mentioned, the breeding stock in Germany was sadly depleted by 1918 and it was not until 1922 that any real recovery was made. This year produced two outstanding brothers, the better of which, according to Philipp Gruenig, was Ari v. Sigalsburg. Not only was he superbly made but, until his transfer to the United States, produced some excellent progeny. Unfortunately, he died soon after crossing the Atlantic, so the Americans did not reap the full benefit of his blood lines.

However, a gradual improvement in general quality was made in Germany over the next three or four years when, suddenly, because of the growing popularity of the breed in the U.S.A., several Americans descended upon the German breeders, and once again during 1926, using the mighty dollar, acquired many of the best dogs in that country. Still, the Germans did retain a few of the best Dobermanns and, with their usual thoroughness and skill as selective breeders, continued to produce several outstanding dogs and bitches over the next few years. Among these was the very refined Modern v. Simmenau, which also eventually went to America and which by many folk was considered one of the best dogs ever to be born in Europe.

Another export was the black dog Troll v. Engelsburg, which, after a successful show career in Germany, also went across the ocean, where he set up many records as a show dog.

And so we come to what I consider the greatest Dobermann of them all. This was the black bitch Jessy v. Sonnenhoehe, which won the Sieger title in Germany in two successive years, whelped outstanding progeny and then went to the U.S.A. She had a superb conformation, excellent reach of neck, beautifully balanced body, was completely feminine in outline, but according to reports was of such a fiery temperament that she took quite a lot of handling.

As I have already said, this breed is of German origin and it is not unnatural that the first breed standard was drawn up in that country. It was in 1899 that Otto Goeller, having improved on the stock left by Louis Dobermann, organised the National Dobermann Pinscher Club, and one year later he and other enthusiasts drew up their standard. Official recognition by the German Kennel Club was immediately obtained.

Apart from a change in height and one or two minor alterations, mainly relating to conformation, there has been little change in the standard adopted in all countries from that formed in the early days in Germany. Of course, type has changed, but this is really a matter of taste and cannot be reflected in a breed standard, neither can it easily be put into words.

Since those not-too-distant days breeders from all over the world have had much pleasure and many thrills when developing the breed into the magnificent animal we know today.

Firm dyed-in-the-wool breeders have occasionally attacked me for saying that it is inevitable that a change in type must take place in dogs, claiming that the original standard for any breed must be strictly adhered to because that was the intention of those who evolved the breed. What these folk cannot and will not see is that everything, including humans and animals, must slowly change over the years, particularly because of modern ideas, fashion and the aesthetic sense that is inherent in most of us. My short answer to those few who decry the modern Dobermann and attempt to make comparisons between those of the 1900s and the dogs of the 1970s is that I, and surely they, prefer the beautiful woman or attractive male we see at present to the types who pleased our ancestors of the stone age. Maybe this comparison is a little far-fetched, nevertheless the difference in time between the stone age and the twentieth century can reasonably be compared with the shorter period in which dogs have been domesticated.

This, of course, has been the case with the Dobermann and because of these changes the standard has been altered in most countries two or three times. In the next chapter I will deal with the standard in Britain, which is little different from those in other countries.

To revert to the history of the breed, we find that the first Dobermanns to enter the United States round about 1908 were no doubt carefully selected for their beauty and brain power and, as I have had the pleasure of seeing many dog shows in the U.S.A. and had the honour of judging Dobermanns several times in that country, I can honestly say that the Americans have greatly improved the breed since its inception and are to be congratulated on their achievements. Dedicated enthusiasts, among whom were the late Mr. Bornstein and the late Mr. Fleitmann, continued the good work by importing such lovely animals as Jessy v. Sonnenhoehe, Waldo v.d. Wachtparade, Artus v. Furstenlager, Troll v. Engelsburg, and it is from stock such as this that almost all the top American Dobermanns of today are descended.

DOBERMANNS IN GERMANY, THE U.S.A. AND EUROPE

It was about this time that a deviation in type appeared in the two main areas of Doberdom, Europe continuing to produce the more solid working type of dog, while 3,000 miles away on the continent of America development of a more refined and elegant type was being made. This condition continued until a few years ago when the Germans, in particular, started to recognise that a working dog could also be an animal of beauty, and mainly through the efforts of Herr Palmer of Furstenfeld fame we started to see Dobermanns with a reach of neck, clean heads, very good fronts and correct angulation.

Let us now look at the development of the breed in both these areas and first consider the European type. William Schmidt, who was a great authority on the breed way back in the 1940s, made much research over a long period and tells us that each year produced one or two outstanding exhibits. As far back as 1898, which was only a few years after Herr Dobermann had started to produce his own type of dog, his successor Otto Goeller owned Graf Belling v. Thueringen which sired quite a number of Sieger winners. Apparently, Otto Goeller was dominant as a breeder of what in those days were considered first-class Dobermanns, and over the next few years he exhibited and won well with the bitch Ulrich's Glocke v. Thueringen, which, in turn, produced the brown Sieger Hellegraf v. Thueringen. Graf Belling and Hellegraf were considered to be outstanding specimens, both were used extensively at stud, and both transmitted good bodies and temperament to their offspring. Hellegraf in particular added nobility and elegance to the breed and stabilised the type then being produced. I learn that this dog's strength as a sire was because of his ability to produce Dobermanns of outstanding gait which, in my opinion, has been lost to a great degree in many present-day German-bred dogs.

Another brown dog that scored extremely well at the time Hellegraf was being exhibited was the upstanding and elegant Junker Hans v. der Ronneburg. It is as well to mention at this stage that both black and brown exhibits competed on equal terms, whereas today, because of the difference in quality and even in build, the two colours do not compete against each other for the Sieger title. In Europe, but not in the United States, or in Britain, there is quite a difference in quality between the two colours and, apart from one or two outstanding examples, the browns are not of the quality of the blacks.

By 1904, Sieger Leporello v. Main made an appearance, and here again we had a taller and more refined type of Dobermann than had previously been seen in Germany. It was claimed that although Leporello deviated from the standard, nobody could resist his elegant appearance and the Sieger title could not be withheld from him. Undoubtedly it was because of the emergence of dogs such as Junker Hans and Leporello that the Germans had to alter their ideas of what constituted the ideal Dobermann and I seem to think that about this time the standard was amended so that these upstanding, yet noble exhibits became recognised as the type actually required.

However, most dogs of this period had long backs, steep hindquarters, French fronts, heads that were too heavy or too short and stood low on the leg, and it was not until 1906 that Otto Goeller exhibited another outstanding specimen, namely Benno v. Thueringen, which brought added lustre to the breed and to the name of Goeller. A year later Benno's son put in an appearance, followed by Edel v. Ilm-Athen, the product of a kennel that was to make itself felt for several years to come.

The year 1910 gave us several popular dogs, the best of which could have been Prinz Modern v. Ilm-Athen. This tall grandson of Hellegraf was used extensively at stud and was dominant in producing dogs with a good sweep of stifle, tremendous depth of brisket, excellent forehands and long clean necks. This dog has been criticised because his head deviated from the ideal but this fault was subsequently corrected in his progeny by the judicious use of bitches carrying good head type. Because of Prinz Modern's qualities, he should go down in history as one of the greats, probably on equality with Graf Belling and Hellegraf. In any case, from 1910 onwards the overall quality of the breed improved and it was possible to see several outstanding exhibits as distinct from only one or two at the various shows held in Germany.

In 1912 there was a further improvement in type, among which was Troll v. Albtal which exerted a good influence when exported to Holland at an early age.

And so we come to the war years when because of conditions many Dobermanns were put to sleep. Breeding programmes were seriously curtailed and much of the best breeding stock sold to neutral countries at comparatively high prices. These conditions did, of course, assist breeders in Switzerland and Holland and Czechoslovakia and undoubtedly out of the sorrow and pain experienced by German Dobermann enthusiasts some good came to those breeders who purchased their stock.

However, Burschel v. Simmenau, born in 1915, did survive the vicissitudes of the war years and was greatly instrumental in resuscitating the breed when hostilities ceased. He produced a son, Lux v.d. Blankenburg, a daughter, Leddy v. Blankenburg, and a grandson, Alex v.d. Sinohoehe, the first of which, used extensively at stud, has become known as one of the greatest sires of all time in Germany. Because of several transfers of ownership, Burschel sired litters all over Germany and I imagine that his blood can be traced back to almost every exhibit in that country today. Not only Burschel, but his son Lux was involved in many changes in ownership, and it was not until he was four years of age that his potency as a sire became recognised. He was full of Ilm-Athen blood, which helped make him into one of the greatest Dobermanns of his period and which also enabled him to produce such outstanding progeny as Lotte II v. Simmenau, which, in turn, passed on her sire's high qualities. Lux eventually went to the U.S.A. where for a time he produced very good litters, and died in 1931.

In 1921 the Dutch-bred dog registered as Favorit v.d. Koningstad was born. He was a tall upstanding brown dog of a quality that persuaded the owner to exhibit him successfully in Germany and other European countries. Eventually, he also went to the U.S.A. and many of the old stagers in the Dobermann cult consider him as the best sire ever to reach America.

It is fact that after the cessation of hostilities many of the best dogs that remained in Germany were sold at high prices to Army of Occupation American soldiers and others from neutral countries. As a matter of fact, if it were not because of the demand from the German Army for Dobermanns to be used as guard dogs and messenger dogs it is probable that all breeding would have ceased in that part of the world. This would have been an irreparable blow to the Dobermann cult and I doubt whether, but for such a demand, the quality of the breed in Europe would be as high as it is today.

Philipp Gruenig tells us that on the day he was ordered to the front line, eighteen of the half-grown puppies in his kennels had to be put to sleep or died of slow starvation and although he kept his two favourites, both succumbed to malnutrition in 1916. It was because of the lack of food in Germany that many breeders, in order to stay alive themselves and also because of the love they had for their dogs, sold them as pets.

The year 1928 saw a complete novice, Mrs. Bauer of Berlin, purchasing a seven-week puppy simply because it was the most extrovert in the litter. This puppy grew on to be Bessy v. Brandenburg, which by the time she was three years old had become a German Siegerin, after which she, with so many other top specimens, was sold to the U.S.A. Following her successes in Germany, Bessy went Best of Winners at Madison Square, New York.

Hamlet v. Herthasee, sire of Bessy, produced other great dogs, almost all of which qualified excellent and two of which became champions. The quality of this blood line must have been quite outstanding because a son of Bessy's litter sister, registered as Desir v. Glueckswinkel, became the German champion in 1933 and at the same show held in Leipzig the litter sister, Daisy, took the bitch champion title. As was becoming common in those days, Desir also went abroad, this time to Japan.

A couple of years later appeared one of the greatest stud dogs of his period. This was the internationally known Troll v.d. Engelsburg, which produced the outstanding 'F' litter, among which were Ferry v. Rauhfelsen and Freya v. Rauhfelsen. I have already mentioned the dam of this litter, which was the fantastic Jessy v.d. Sonnenhoehe, and it is not surprising that both Ferry and Freya took dog and bitch German champion titles in 1938.

Once again the war years of 1939 to 1945 took their toll of Dobermanns in Germany where breeding was cut to a minimum and many dogs were put to sleep. However, several enthusiasts continued with their kennels and when hostilities ceased, and the American Army of Occupation had purchased many of the best specimens, serious breeding began again.

One of the first new champions was Hasso v.d. Neckarstrasse, which not only won his title in breed competition but also passed every possible working trial including a qualification as a guide dog for the blind. Quite naturally he was in great demand as a stud dog, and among his more successful progeny there appeared Ferry v. Heinrichsburg, which easily became a champion.

Another top kennel at this particular time was Germania, owned by Herr Schneider, who, until 1964, when he died, had become recognised as the most successful breeder for many years. The bitch champion title in 1949 went to his Hella Germania, followed in 1951 and 1952 by Ester Germania with many similar top honours right through to 1964 during which time the blue bitch Adda v. Germania and the black dog Titus v. Germania and the brown bitch Cita Germania all became champions.

Going back a few years we find Herr Felsing founding a kennel under the affix 'Felsingpaff' using a champion dog born in East Germany registered as Boris v. Rehwalde as his main stud dog. Of the many first-class specimens to be born in this kennel we

saw Boris v. Felsingpaff gain the title of champion in 1953,
Carmen v. Felsingpaff taking the bitch title in 1957, with litter
brother and sister Hede v. Felsingpaff and Heide v. Felsingpaff
repeating these successes.

The next most important kennel to emerge was Herr Palmer's
v. Furstenfeld. Using world champion Lump v. Hagenstolz as his
main sire, Herr Palmer produced champions Citta and Citto v.
Furstenfeld, the latter also siring Ch. Ina v. Furstenfeld.

Again going back a few years we remember the 1950 dog
champion Troll v.d. Eversburg, which I think went to Brazil,
while his brother Tasso v.d. Eversburg came over to my own
kennels in England. Other champions of this period were Casso
v. Kleinwaldheim and Etzel v. Romberg, the former bred by
Herr Klein, who at this time was recognised as one of the more
knowledgeable breeders in Germany. Etzel was, of course, bred
by Frau Reiners, well known for breeding brown Dobermanns,
one of which, Tittau Romberg, became champion in 1958.

The next several years have seen the continuing success of Herr
Palmer's v. Furstenfeld kennels and the emergençe of several
others such as Herr Wilking's v. Forell affix, but as I shall deal
with those when bringing this book up to date in a few years'
time, we will content ourselves by having recorded some of the
most successful dogs and kennels from the beginning of the
breed in Germany and switch to what has happened in the U.S.A.
up to the time of importations into England.

It is pointless, I think, to delve back too deeply into the pre-war
years because from 1908 to 1918 the Americans were going
through the same phase as we experienced in Britain from 1947
to 1952 when the breed was almost unknown and few outstanding dogs were to be seen. However, I learn from a most interesting book written by Willie Schmidt that three Germans who had
emigrated to the United States, namely Mr. Herman Meyer of
Philadelphia, Mr. Jaeger of Rochester, and Mr. Vucassovitch of
Boston, were among the first to take Dobermanns into their
country of adoption.

Starting in 1923, the American breeders invited several German
judges to the U.S.A. so that their opinion on progress and quality
could be obtained. Among the earliest of these judges were the

late Peter Umlauff, recognised as one of the leading authorities and whose daughter still takes a great interest in the breed, and that charming character the late Philipp Gruenig, to whom all of us all over the world owe deep gratitude for his works on the breed.

In 1921 the Dobermann Pinscher Club of America was formed, and one year later the Standard as recognised in Germany was adopted. From then on the popularity of the Dobermann increased by leaps and bounds and soon thousands of puppies were being registered from coast to coast. Full detail of the development of the breed up to the end of the Second World War is difficult to trace, so I think it best to begin again at 1945 and then record the present-day era in the United States. I am indebted to Joanna Walker for much of the information and detail contained in this chapter, she having kept records of the main producers in the breed over the past several years. Of course, it is not possible to go too far back into the history of American-bred Dobermanns but a certain amount of research brings out the following.

Coming to the more modern breeders, of whom there are many in the United States, there first leaps to mind Peggy Adamson, who owns the Damasyn Kennels on Long Island. Immediately one thinks of Peggy, who for many years bred both blacks and browns, one is reminded of the great dog Ch. Dictator of Glenhugel, which has probably done more for the breed both in the States and in Britain than any other sire. Unfortunately, I never saw this glorious brown dog, but photographs and his records confirm that he was one of the greatest. In all he sired fifty-two champions, approximately half of which were brown, and other breeders in the U.S.A. claim that he always threw his fantastic type, temperament, character, personality and showmanship to his progeny. There are not many pedigrees in either America or Britain that do not contain the name of Dictator, which only goes to prove that he was really outstanding and appreciated by other breeders.

It is interesting at this time to note that, occasionally, puppies carrying Dictator's blood even as far back as the tenth generation have a slight cowlick up the nape of the neck, which has become known as 'the mark of Dictator'. Maybe one of his greatest sons was Ch. Damasyn the Solitaire, which not only qualified in breed classes but also earned the obedience title of C.D. Ex. This can only prove that enthusiasm such as that possessed by Peggy Adamson can bring out the brains in dogs that win top honours in breed classes. Solitaire also produced many champions and has left his mark on the breed for perpetuity.

Other dominant and well-known kennels on the East Coast are those owned by Ed and Judy Weiss, Monroe and Natalie Stebbins, and Ellen Hoffmann. The Weiss prefix is Ebonaire and many champions have emerged from this kennel. In several cases each litter contained three or four champions, demonstrating that selective and careful breeding must bring excellent results. Chs. Touchdown, Flying Tackle, Touche, Gridiron, and Balesta all made their names at an early age and were extensively used for breeding programmes over several years.

The Stebbinses used an abbreviation of their own name as a prefix and I well remember judging a huge entry of Dobermanns in Chicago where Steb's Top Skipper became best of breed. He was an elegant, yet powerful, showman, full of character and temperament, which has undoubtedly been passed on to his progeny. Currently Steb, as Monroe is affectionately known in the Dobermann world, is an American Kennel Club field representative and up to a few years ago delighted in showing puppies that had been sold to other exhibitors and that had been sired by his own stud dogs. There is no doubt at all that the name of Ch. Steb's Top Skipper will long remain in Dobermann history, his blood having been extensively used over something like eight years.

I would imagine that Ellen Hoffman must be about the smallest handler of Dobermanns anywhere in the world, but, believe me, her short stature is more than compensated for by her great heart. She is a mine of information, always willing to help novice handlers and breeders and has enjoyed much success in the show rings with her Elfred kennels. Ch. Elfred Spark Plug proved to be one of the great dogs in Doberdom and produced quite a few champions. A record of dogs and breeders on the East Coast would not be complete without mentioning Jane Kay once owner of the world-famous Kay-Hills Kennels. She is now recognised as one of the best judges of Dobermanns and several other working breeds in the U.S.A. and is a fund of knowledge

Anne Hewitt

Ch. Tavey's Stormy Achievement

Sally Anne Thompson

Sonata of Tavey

German and American Ch. bitch Jessy v.d. Sonnenhoehe, 1934

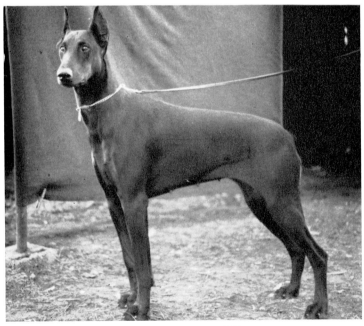

Citta vom Furstenfeld

Anne Hewitt

Ch. Edencourt's Avenger

Anne Hewitt

Ch. Annastock Lance

Auldrigg Corvette

Diane Pearce

Ch. Tavey's Stormy Medallion and Hensel Midnight Max

willingly imparted to other Dobermaniacs.

Moving away from the East Coast towards Pennsylvania we find Tess Hensler's kennels carrying the affix Von Ahrtal. Something like sixty breed champions have been bred by Tess, but not content with this, she has concentrated on obedience competition, working many dogs to their titles. Perhaps this excellent breeder is best known for her team of obedience-trained dogs that regularly give demonstrations at the larger shows throughout the States.

Ch. Felix v. Ahrtal was no doubt the top producing sire from these kennels, his total of champion progeny exceeding twenty-two.

Other well-known kennels in that particular area are the Highbriar, Toledobe and Tedell, all in Ohio, and all, especially in this present day and age, producing top-class Dobermanns. One of the record-breaking dogs from this area was, of course, Ch. Singenwald's Prince Kuhio, owned by Dale Rickert, with whom, and his professional handler George Rood, I have spent many happy hours. Dale is now deceased, as also is Kuhio, and although Mrs. Rickert carried on the kennels for some time, no breeding has continued.

Let us now wander a little further away into what is known as the mid-West of the United States. Here we find Jack and Eleanor Brown, whose surname is always given to Dobermanns bred in their kennels. How wise they were when seeking a foundation bitch a couple of decades ago to purchase a Dictator daughter, which became the beautiful Ch. Dow's Dame of Kilburn. She was mated to some of the top dogs of that period, among which were Alcor Emperor and also to her sire, the last-named producing a couple of well-known champions in Ch. Brown's Eric and Ch. Brown's Evangeline. Eric was retired from the show ring after attaining the title of champion, was placed at stud, and became one of America's greatest and most dominant sires. One of his daughters, Brown's Bridget, was, when born, the runt of the litter and was of such a sickly condition that she was taken to the veterinary surgeon to be put to sleep. The Browns, hearing of the fate in store for such a well-bred Dobermann, collected her from the veterinary surgeon and with tender care and their skill in raising puppies built her up both in body and confidence until

B

the time came when she became a champion. She went on to make near records in the breed, but, unfortunately, did not leave behind more than one champion.

Other high-class and best-in-show winning Dobermanns did emerge from this kennel and I would be at fault if it were not recorded that the Browns' kennels were among the most dominant of their time.

A few years after the Browns had laid the foundation of their kennels Keith and Joanna Walker purchased the lovely brown bitch Ch. Damasyn the Waltzing Brook C.D. and mated her to Brown's Eric. This mating was certainly a clever move because from the resultant litter there appeared Ch. Derek of Marks Tey and Ch. Dodie of Marks Tey, both of which were extremely successful in the show ring. Derek, as a matter of fact, sired many champions before passing away in 1968.

It is interesting to note that the affix of Marks Tey is derived from a village of that name in Essex, England, which was Joanna's birthplace.

Maybe the Dobermann that attracted the most publicity for the breed was Ch. Borong the Warlock, which was shown relentlessly all over the States, Canada and Cuba. This dog, the constant companion of Henry Frampton, also went over to Germany, where, for some unknown reason, his high qualities were not fully realised. He won innumerable best of breeds, groups, and best in shows all over America and when his owner died round about 1967 he was put to sleep and both were cremated together. Mrs. Theodosia Frampton is still active in the breed and the day may arrive when another exhibit of a quality equal to Borong the Warlock may make its appearance in the show ring. Incidentally, this dog also won several qualifications in obedience work, which could prove the devotion both dog and master had towards each other.

Going now completely over to the West Coast, we come across the well-known Rancho Dobes kennels owned and run by Vivienne and Brint Edwards. It was here that Ch. Rancho Dobe's Storm was born, sent across to Len Carey in New York and handled through to best in show Westminster on two successive occasions by that expert Pete Knoop. Storm was a son of Ch.

Primo, which, in turn, was a son of Ch. Alcor, all three being recorded as among the most outstanding Dobermanns of their era. The Rancho Dobes kennels have produced a great number of champions, but recently, due to ill health, the owners have had to cut back on their activities.

It seems to me that in California there are more active kennels than anywhere else in the U.S.A. which could account for what appears to be the superiority of the breed in that part of the country. One of the most magnificent specimens I have ever seen was the lovely black bitch Ch. Ru-Mars Tsushima C.D., known to everybody affectionately as 'Tish', and which was almost un-beatable during her short show career. It was a great tragedy when in 1968 while whelping a litter this beautiful Dobermann died, and the loss to the breed is incalculable.

However, Ron and Margaret Carveth, owners of the Ru-Mar affix, have continued to produce extremely good Dobermanns and it is quite on the cards that their skill and devotion will one day enable them exhibit another of the same calibre as Tish.

Still thinking of the Californian Dobermanns, my mind jumps to some of the newer kennels, in particular those carrying the prefixes of Haydenhill, Westwind, and Marienburg. The latter, owned by Mary Rodgers Shea, owns Ch. Sultana v. Marienburg, which not only became the top winning Dobermann in 1967 but has, in addition, twice won best of breed at the Dobermann Pinscher Club of America Annual Specialty Show. This is no easy feat when it is remembered that upwards of 500 exhibits are entered at this annual event.

Of course, there are other important kennels all over the States, as there are also many other great dogs and bitches, but having given the names and records of those who stick in my memory and about which a certain amount of research has been made, I will finish this chapter saying that both numerically and in quality the Americans, because of their love of the breed and due to the fact that they think nothing of travelling a couple of thousand miles in order to use the stud dog they consider best for their bitches, have attained a peak in the breed that cannot be equalled anywhere in the world.

At about the same time as the Americans began to appreciate

the Dobermann, other intelligent folk in countries nearer to the land of origin began to import and breed Dobermanns. The Dutch, Scandinavians, French and Swiss purchased good blood lines from the Germans and quite soon produced some very good specimens. Mrs. Knijff Dermout of Holland, in particular, built a most impressive strain and in my opinion has been for many years one of the most dominant and successful exhibitors on the Continent of Europe.

DOBERMANNS IN GREAT BRITAIN

It was not until 1947 that serious importation into Britain began. Mrs. Curnow and I, having seen and learned to admire the Dobermann during our travels in Europe, were persuaded by the late Leo Wilson to launch the breed in England. At the same time, Lionel Hamilton Renwick bought a couple of Dobermanns in whelp, but, unfortunately, both he and we had the great misfortune to lose almost all of the litters in quarantine. This was a serious blow at the outset, but we enthusiasts were not daunted by such ill luck, and other importations were arranged. Here, again, the importers had the good sense to buy bitches from well-known kennels in Germany and Holland and had them mated to some of the top dogs carrying the best blood in their respective countries.

These first importations caused much comment among the general dog public, some having heard or read that the Dobermann had an unreliable temperament. I well remember the late Phyllis Robson writing a scathing article in a dog magazine asking why I had to import another German breed reputed to be vicious, and I can also remember my reply, which was to the effect that the country of origin did not matter and that a dog often reflected the temperament of its owner. After all, many of us prefer Turkish carpets to those made in England and many of like discrimination prefer Swiss watches to those produced in Japan or Russia.

During 1947 twenty-four keen admirers, among whom were some of our foremost judges, and others who had learned to recognise the qualities of the breed while serving in the Middle

East and Europe during the Second World War, founded the Dobermann Pinscher Club, which immediately received Kennel Club recognition. From then on the Dobermann has gone from strength to strength and is now among the more popular breeds of working dogs in Britain.

During the first ten or twelve years after the Dobermann Club was formed the main imports came from Germany and Holland and among these were:

Derb v. Brunoberg	Vilja Germania
Beka v. Brunoberg	Ditta v. Scholzbach
Bruno v. Ehrgarten	Timo v.d. Brunoberg
Prinses Anja v't Scheepjeskerk	Treu v.d. Steinfurthohe
Iris v. Wellborn	Centa v. Empsperle
Angela v. Kastanienhof	Ritter v.d. Heerhof
Wilm v. Forell	Ulf v. Margarethenhof
Bill v. Blauenblut	Donathe v. Begertal
Pia v. Dobberhof	Gin v. Forell
Tasso v.d. Eversburg	Britta v.d. Heerhof
Roeanka v.d. Rhederveld	Astor v.d. Morgensonne
Waldox v. Aamsveen	Alex v. Rodenaer

Perhaps the most interesting of these dogs was Ulf v. Margarethenhof, a solid, noble creature brought over to England by an American serviceman. After Ulf—Peter to his friends—had been in quarantine for about three months the owner telephoned me and asked whether I would care to take the dog over free of any charge. Such a surprising offer prompted me to ask the reason for such generosity and I was informed that Peter was too sharp to handle. At that time I did not wish to be saddled with a dog that could not be fully trusted so I telephoned the late Sergeant Harry Darbyshire, the renowned police-dog handler, and asked whether he was interested in having the dog.

Harry's immediate reaction was to visit the quarantine kennels, where he promptly got bitten, following which the dog received a good hiding and eventually, when released from the kennels, went to the Surrey Constabulary. An incredible and lasting affection grew up between trainer and dog and a year or so later Peter became the first-ever Dobermann to become a working trials champion. This dog was used extensively at stud and sired many excellent working-type Dobermanns, most of which found their way to other constabularies.

Derb v. Brunoberg also had a most successful career as a stud dog in those early days and it was one of his progeny, Alpha of Tavey, born in 1948, which formed the basis of Eva Would's kennels. Bruno of Tavey, which was born in quarantine, soon became one of the most prepotent sires, producing, in conjunction with the Dutch bitch Prinses Anja v't Scheepjeskerk, most of the early champions.

Among the foremost of these were Ch. Elegant of Tavey, the first-ever bitch championship certificate winner and Ch. and Obedience Ch. Jupiter of Tavey which still today holds the record of being the only dual champion Dobermann in Great Britain.

Reverting to the original imports, Lionel Hamilton Renwick brought in a couple of bitches in whelp and it was one of these, Britta v.d. Heerhof, which started the Birling kennels and produced several winning exhibits such as Birling Rebel, Birling Rogue, and Birling Rachel. Perhaps Tasso v. d. Eversburg deserves mention as a dominant sire because this grand dog I imported from Germany gave us several champions in Lyric of Tavey, Lustre of Tavey, Precept of Tavey, Pilot of Tavey and that marvellous working-trials bitch Lorelei of Tavey. It was, I think, because of Lorelei's prowess when in the hands of Jean Faulks that the working side of Dobermanns was fully recognised by others who were keen in this particular field and encouraged them to buy and train similarly bred animals.

These continental blood lines did much to help put the breed on the map in Britain and eventually were followed by Kitty v. Wellborn and several others.

The judicious mixture of blood in all these Dobermanns has resulted in the high quality we see today. Not only in breed competition do we see excellent results because in club working tests, Kennel Club working trials and also in general obedience competition, we know of brilliant performances put up by Hawk of Trevellis, Gurnard Gloomy Sunday, Lorelei of Tavey, Dollar Premium, Tavey's Stormy Jael, Yuba Adonis, Dandy of Dovecote, Jupiter of Tavey and many others.

In general obedience competition we had among many consistent performers such exhibits as Maverick the Brave, Ch. Tavey's Stormy Master, Heiner Rustic, Annastock Moonraker, and Dudley Wontner Smith's two bitches.

Maybe the repetition of all these names will bore some readers, but I must point out that these dogs will go down in history as the foundation of the breed in Britain and it is just as well to record them.

Much has happened over the past years, not the least of which is that we British breeders have dispelled the idea that Dobermanns are vicious and unreliable, and a great improvement in quality both with regard to beauty and working ability has taken place.

It will, of course, be easily understood after breeding for a few years with the restricted number of blood lines imported from Europe that new stock had to be introduced in order to maintain and improve the quality already in Britain. With this in mind, my wife and I, during 1954, imported two bitches from the U.S.A., had them mated to the two top stud dogs of their time, namely Am. Ch. Rancho Dobe's Storm and Am. Ch. Steb's Top Skipper and enjoyed the good fortune of rearing excellent litters after the puppies left the quarantine kennels at the age of six weeks.

These were followed by several other bitches and one stud dog from America, enabling us and other serious breeders in Britain to continue with sensible breeding programmes. Margaret Bastable and David Kingsberry also imported stock from Germany, so at the present time there are over here ample blood lines with which to work and improve the high quality that exists today.

It is obvious that Dobermanns are now much better known by the general public, that there is a demand for puppies and that serious breeders are able to produce good stock. In Britain there has been a steady advance in registrations with the Kennel Club and the figures given in Appendix A show the numbers of puppies registered since 1951.

To demonstrate the great strides in type and quality of the breed over recent years I need only quote a few of the exhibits that have put up excellent records. The first-ever champion in England was Ch. Elegant of Tavey, a bitch of all German blood lines and which was never beaten after winning her first certificate at Cruft's in 1952. Next, during the following year, we had Jupiter of Tavey, which, after becoming a breed champion when just out of puppyhood, went on to qualify as an obedience champion, thus becoming the only dual champion Dobermann in Great Britain.

Another litter born in quarantine contained that great producer Ch. Acclamation of Tavey, which at the moment of writing has sired twenty-one champions. In between times we had Ch. Precept of Tavey, which gained his crown at a very tender age and in the same litter there was Ch. Pilot of Tavey which won his title in South Africa. More recently in the show ring we have seen such record-breaking Dobermanns as Ch. Tavey's Stormy Wrath, winner of 17 challenge certificates and 6 best in show awards and Ch. Iceberg of Tavey, which holds 33 challenge certificates and 22 best-in-show wins. All of these were, of course, bred in the Tavey kennels, as were also Chs. Oberan of Tavey, Tavey's Stormy Willow, Opinion of Tavey, and others.

Betty Harris (*née* Hoxey) who was one of the more serious breeders, has produced Chs. Tumlow Impeccable, Tumlow Katrina, Tumlow Storm Caesar and Tumlow Fantasy, some of which have left their mark on the breed as it is today. Jane and Greg Parkes apply serious thought to their breeding programme, as does also Alf Hogg, and among them they have produced Ch. Annastock Lance, Ch. Triogen Traffic Cop, and other very good specimens. Eva Would, with her very small kennel of Dobermanns, has been extremely successful over the past twenty years, producing Ch. Claus of Cartergate, Ch. Day of Cartergate, Ch. Daybreak of Cartergate, Ch. Caprice of Cartergate and Ch. Helena of Cartergate, and it is only because of ill health, which has cut down her breeding programme, that this popular breeder has not had more success over the past few years.

In Scotland, where, because of the difficulties of travelling, breeding programmes have been a little difficult, we have had a few outstanding exhibits, among them being Chs. Carrickgreen Confederate, Crontham King, Clanguard Comanche, Auldrigg Corsair and Clanguard Cadet. Of course, there are and have been other champion exhibits, but to enumerate them all would take much time and research. Sufficient it is to say that as the years have gone on the quality in Dobermanns has improved and, as I have already said, the day will surely come when there are many really outstanding dogs in this country.

Harking back to the beginning of this chapter and realising that Louis Dobermann set out to build the dog of his own personal choice, it will be realised that my oft-repeated statement that our breed was 'tailor made' is no idle comment.

Thinking over my comments on Dobermanns abroad and realising that we in Britain have a comparatively short experience with the breed, I think that congratulations are due to exhibitors for the wonderful progress so far made.

A definite type running fairly true to standard is being generally produced, which fact has been repeatedly noted by foreign judges who have honoured us by officiating at championship shows. It is true that one or two of these visiting judges have commented on the small proportion of our Dobermanns that have a missing tooth, tan markings that are not a really deep colour, eyes that could be darker, and the tan markings on the chest too large. While I am not overlooking the gravity of what is supposed to be progressive deterioration, the terrific emphasis placed by some continental judges on these particular fetishes does not greatly influence me. As a matter of fact, it has been shown that the proportion of British-bred Dobermanns with one or more missing teeth is no higher and possibly lower than those bred in the U.S.A. and on the Continent.

Lightish eyes and light tan markings can also be found in the U.S.A. and Germany, although in the latter country Dobermanns carrying these faults do not often appear in the show ring, the owners knowing full well that the exhibit will be heavily penalised. It would be wrong of me to say that it does not matter if a Dobermann has a missing tooth or markings that are not of a deep shade, because, after all, these are faults, but what I do want to emphasise is that all faults must be assessed according to their gravity, as must all good points to their relative value.

This brings me to the subject of selective breeding. Like does not breed like when dealing with dogs any more than it does with human beings. A champion sire does not always breed a champion in his progeny and the reverse is often the case. One particular dog, now dead, which shall be nameless and which, due to a period spent in quarantine kennels, followed by an attack of distemper while still a youngster, was nevertheless, because of his bloodlines, used quite a lot in this country and produced several really outstanding champions. Selective and line-breeding is a study in itself and it is not my intention to write on this subject. However, I would say that careful selection given to the use of a sire based primarily on progeny which has been produced with a bitch similarly bred as your own can have only good results.

It was, as far as my memory serves me, in 1952 that the Dobermann Club had the pleasure of having Philipp Gruenig, the world-renowned authority on the breed, over here in England to judge. It was a great thrill to hear him say, at a dinner given in his honour, that several of our exhibits, in particular Ch. Elegant of Tavey, could compete with those in Germany.

Jumping a few years, I can well remember the visits of other continental judges, such as the German Willi Hirscher and the Norwegian expert, the late Julius Selikowitz, both of whom congratulated British breeders on the way in which the breed had progressed.

And so slowly and steadily the breed was becoming better recognised and appreciated by the general public and after the first championship certificates were awarded by the Kennel Club in 1952 a marked increase in registrations was noted. A couple of years later, having made regular business trips to the U.S.A., my wife and I decided to introduce American blood lines into Britain, hoping to add a little refinement to what has become known as the continental type.

It is no overstatement to claim that the litter born to Am. Ch. Rustic Adagio, sired by Ch. Rancho Dobe's Storm the fantastic twice best-in-show winner of Westminster (which is the equivalent to our Cruft's) revolutionised the breed in Britain. In this litter were five puppies, all, of course, born in quarantine and all five, which rejoiced in the names of Abundance, Achievement, Adagio, Acacia and Accolade, became champions, Accolade in Australia. It was when these exhibits, in particular Abundance and Achievement, were shown in competition that best-in-show all breeds awards were gained and once again there was an upsurge in public interest which brought into the Dobermann cult some of our most successful breeders of today.

From Europe we had a few more importations, one of them being the bitch Kitty v. Wellborn owned by David Kingsberry. Such was the position round about 1958 when kennels owned by Eva Would, Alf Hogg, Greg Parkes, Philippa Thorne Dunn, Dorothy Horton, Margaret Bastable, Mrs. Curnow, Elizabeth Harris and, more latterly, by Jean Ryan, were judiciously mixing blood lines from Europe and the U.S.A. to the benefit of the breed in general.

2

Conformation and Character

BEFORE considering the conformation of a Dobermann, around which of course the standard is built, we must remember that almost all the detail contained therein is concerned with the skeleton, muscles, skin and coat. Movement is controlled by the skeleton and muscles, while the general appearance is enhanced or otherwise by the addition and condition of skin and coat.

Now let us look at the standard as approved by the Kennel Club and try to see, in greater detail, what exactly is required.

> The Dobermann is a dog of good medium size with a well-set body, muscular and elegant.
> He has a proud carriage and a bold, alert temperament. His form is compact and tough and, owing to his build, capable of great speed. His gait is light and elastic. His eyes show intelligence and firmness of character, and he is loyal and obedient.

Although the above description of a Dobermann gives a general picture of the breed, it must be remembered that the expression 'of good medium size' means exactly what it says and, when taken in conjunction with the section dealing with the body, dogs which are palpably over or under size should be penalised.

Some judges, having in mind that the Dobermann is actually a working dog, prefer the heavier type of animal, forgetting that the standard asks for elegance. An elegant dog can still be muscular, whereas many with very heavy muscle formation are far from elegant. We should not forget that the breed must be able to work and, in particular, track for the whole twenty-four hours of the day if necessary, and I doubt very much indeed if the heavy flabby type could carry his weight for that period. Again, the

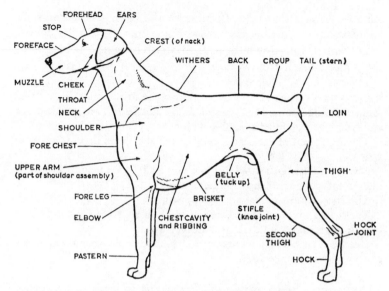

FIG. 1   Anatomy of the Dobermann

standard calls for a light and elastic gait which cannot be attained unless there is elegance in the animal. This tailor-made dog—and remember he was evolved from other quite well-known breeds with the intention of producing an aristocrat—must be a figure of geometric harmony. Pride and alertness are absolutely essential, but these qualities are not to be confused with viciousness, which is a serious fault.

It is not always possible or easy to evaluate correctly the qualities in a Dobermann while he is being exhibited in the show ring. Some judges interpret boldness and an alert temperament in a way that asks for the dog to be aggressive and fierce. This should not be so, and in my opinion the way to assess such traits is to see whether the dog stands up to examination with no flinching or fear showing in his eyes. Remember, however, that a Dobermann, as with most other guard dogs, has a natural aversion to strangers, not necessarily taking to them at first sight. Such aversion should not penalise the dog, whereas continued retreating from examination or running behind the handler does prove that the animal is not bold. Any sign of fear must, of course, be penalised. If the exhibit shows little or no affection for the judge, this should not be mistaken for fear because it is also true that the handler, whose temperament runs down the lead, may also have little affection for the judge himself and *vice versa*.

HEAD AND SKULL: Has to be proportionate to the body. It must be long, well filled under the eyes and clean cut. Its form seen from above and from the side must resemble a blunt wedge.

The upper part of the head should be as flat as possible and free from wrinkle.

The top of the skull should be flat with a slight stop, and the muzzle line extend parallel to the top line of the skull.

The cheeks must be flat and the lips tight.

The nose should be solid black in black dogs, solid dark brown in brown dogs, and solid dark grey in blue dogs.

Head out of balance in proportion to body, dish-faced, snipey or cheeky should be penalised.

As in every breed, we find Dobermanns with various forms of head, some too heavy, usually because of thick cheek formation, and others too fine, mainly because of weak, thin and snipey muzzles. Our standard best sums up the ideal when asking for a blunt wedge when viewed from the side and above, as shown in Fig. 2. Incorrect head types are shown in Figs. 3 and 4, Fig. 3 being too snipey and Fig. 4 too heavy in skull, Fig. 4 also showing a lot of dewlap.

The slight stop referred to in the standard is that part of the head where the skull meets the upper jaw. There should be no distinct stop but rather a slope as shown in Fig. 1, and the top line of the skull should be parallel to the top line of muzzle. The length of the skull when measured from the occiput to the eyes should be approximately equal to the length of muzzle when measured from eyes to tip of nose. Quite a few Dobermanns in Britain, and all over the world, for that matter, carry too much loose skin around the mouth, thus giving a sour and sad expression to the head.

Some folk will tell you that the larger the cranium in a dog, the larger and therefore the better is the brain. This, of course, is nonsense and is easily disproved when comparing the size of the skull

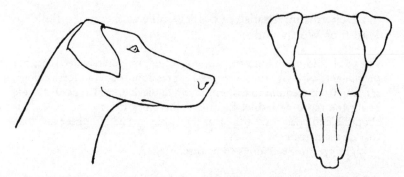

FIG. 2   Correct head: 'blunt wedge'

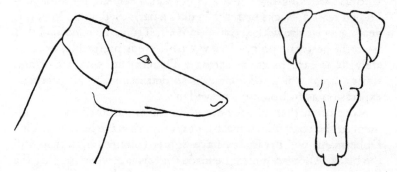

FIG. 3   Incorrect head: too snipey

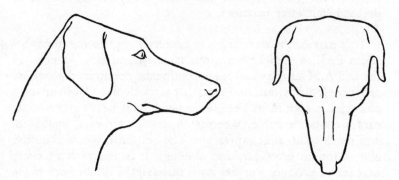

FIG. 4   Incorrect head: too heavy in skull

in a Dobermann, Alsatian or Border Collie with that of a Bulldog, Mastiff or Wolfhound.

EYES: Should be almond-shaped, not round, moderately deep set, not prominent, with vigorous, energetic expression. Iris of uniform colour, ranging from medium to darkest brown in black dogs, the darker shade being the more desirable. In browns or blues the colour of the iris should blend with that of the markings, but not be of lighter hue than that of the markings.

Light eyes in black dogs to be discouraged.

Light eyes, it is maintained, spoil the expression and, while this is true, we must keep in mind the contention held by enthusiasts who use working dogs that a light-eyed specimen, for some unknown reason, tracks better than does a dark-eyed dog. However, dealing as we are with show specimens, it must be conceded that from the aesthetic point of view a dark eye is preferable. Fortunately, it is rare to come across a Dobermann with round and staring eyes, which, of course, is so detrimental to an energetic expression as to become a grave fault.

More often than not the eye colour is determined by the pigment in the coat, which means, of course, that the brown or blue Dobermann will invariably have lighter-coloured eyes than will the black. Allowance must be made for this fact when judging the lighter-coloured dogs.

EARS: Should be small, neat and set high on the head. Erect or dropped, but erect preferred.

This part of the standard was expressly kept in this form because English-bred Dobermanns have natural ears, whereas in the U.S.A., Germany and some continental countries the ears are cropped. It is obvious, however, that as much of the Dobermann's character is seen in its head, long pendulous, heavy and low-set ears are not desirable, whereas small high-set ears, well-used, add much to an alert expression. The Standard, you will notice, allows for an erect ear, and although it is the wish of every breeder to produce puppies with this asset, I doubt very much whether it will ever be attained.

In Norway there was a bitch with natural pricked ears, and although she was mated back to her father in an attempt to fix this trait, the experiment failed.

MOUTH: Should be very well developed, solid and strong, with a scissor bite. The incisors of the lower jaw must touch the inner face of the incisors of the upper jaw.

Overshot or undershot mouths, badly arranged or decayed teeth to be penalised.

It will be noticed that no mention is made of the number of teeth required, although this is quoted in most continental standards for Dobermanns. The Germans, in particular, insist that unless a Dobermann has all forty-two teeth he should be disqualified from a major prize, no matter how perfect the animal may be elsewhere. This, I think, is carrying perfection a little too far and I would rather have a dog with forty-one teeth correctly set in his head than one with forty-two teeth in an over- or undershot mouth.

To further illustrate this point, I know of an exhibit in Germany which had one missing pre-molar in the lower jaw and one pre-molar too many in the upper jaw. It was decided by the German judges that the mouth was correct because the full total of forty-two teeth were in existence, whereas I claim that the mouth had two definite faults.

Some people maintain that missing teeth is a degenerate fault and likely to worsen from generation to generation, but against this is the established fact that many skeletons of wolves, and remember they are closely allied to the canine race, found in conditions which prove them to be at least 2,000 years old, had missing pre-molars. Many generations have been born since then and wolves today have no more missing teeth than had their predecessors.

The correct Dobermann dentition is best described as a scissor bite, which is illustrated in Fig. 5(a), this giving a very powerful grip. It is not often one comes across a Dobermann with over- or undershot jaws, but Figs. 5(b) and (c) are given to illustrate these faults. A further faulty tooth formation is shown in Fig. 5(d), this being referred to as a pincer bite.

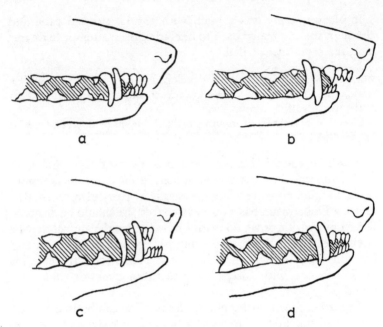

Fig. 5   Dentition: (a) Correct scissor bite   (b) Overshot jaw
(c) Undershot jaw   (d) Pincer bite

NECK: Should be fairly long and lean, carried erect and with considerable nobility, slightly convex and proportionate to the whole shape of the dog.

The region of the nape has to be muscular.

Dewlap and loose skin are undesirable.

This is the part of the body that can add to or detract from elegance; a graceful long and slightly arched neck flowing into the top line of the body in one rhythmic sweep is not only pleasing to the eye but proves correct shoulder placement. Quite a few Dobermanns, although having a very good neck, are spoilt because upright shoulders give the appearance of a 'stuck on' neck with a distinct break where it enters the topline of the body. *See* Figs. 8(a) and (b).

Dewlap or bagginess of the skin under the neck as shown in

Fig. 4 is a definite fault, because much of the graceful line is spoilt by this condition. Stuffy necks, that is to say short and thick, are most ungainly, here again showing lack of elegance and grace.

It must be remembered that a Dobermann is a tracking dog, and therefore needs a reach of neck in order to get his head close to the ground. If he were a sled dog or an animal bred expressly for pulling carts, a short thick neck would be the ideal. However, the Dobermann is certainly no slave, such as are many sled dogs, so a longish elegant neck is desirable.

FOREQUARTERS: The shoulder blade and upper arm should meet at an angle of 90 degrees. Relative length of shoulder and upper arm should be as one, excess length of upper arm being much less undesirable than excess length of shoulder blade.

The legs, seen from the front and side, are perfectly straight and parallel to each other from elbow to pastern, muscled and sinewy, with round bone proportionate to body structure. In a normal position and when gaiting, the elbow should lie close to the brisket.

I should comment on the stipulated 90-degree angle between the shoulder blade and upper arm. Philipp Gruenig and Julius Selikowitz, both now dead, two of the most knowledgeable judges of Dobermanns, have said during the past few years that an angle of 100 degrees is all one can reasonably expect in such a square animal, and from my own point of view I have found that the best-moving dogs do not have the ideal as set out in the standard. Of course, upright shoulders will most certainly give an incorrect gait and must be penalised. No mention is made of the muscle formation in this section of the standard, so do remember that a Dobermann must be well muscled along the upper arm and shoulders, but not to a degree that gives a coarse overloaded appearance. It will be found that a dog with soft muscles, especially those between the elbow and brisket, does not move soundly, giving the well-known 'loose elbows' effect. A Dobermann in good hard condition will have its muscle formation clearly visible, whereas a soft or over-fat animal will not. Keep in mind also that the chest must be broad and capacious, with sufficient space to take the heart and lungs, which are so essential for stamina. The point of the breast bone should stand out in front of the chest just

a little, but not so exaggerated that it gives the appearance of a
chicken breast. It will invariably be found that a Dobermann with
no prominence of chest is straight in shoulder or too long in
upper arm, thus destroying the 100-degree angle which is essential
if the dog is to move freely and correctly (Fig. 6).

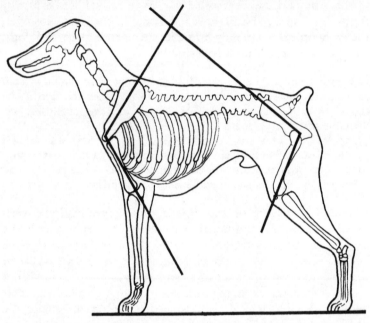

FIG. 6   Straight in shoulder, too long in upper arm

Bow-legged or 'Chippendale' legs, as shown in Figs. 7 (b) and
(c), must be penalised, both showing inherent weaknesses, incorrect feeding or lack of exercise.

BODY: Should be square, height measured vertically from the ground
to the highest point of the withers, equalling the length measured
horizontally, from the forechest to rear projection of the upper thigh.

The back should be short and firm with the topline sloping slightly
from the withers to the croup, the female, needing room to carry
litters, may be slightly longer in the loin.

The belly should be fairly well tucked up.

Ribs should be deep and well-sprung, reaching to elbow.
Long, weak or roach backs to be discouraged.

Here we come to what makes or mars a real Dobermann. Fig.
8(a) will demonstrate the ideal, showing the flow of neck into the

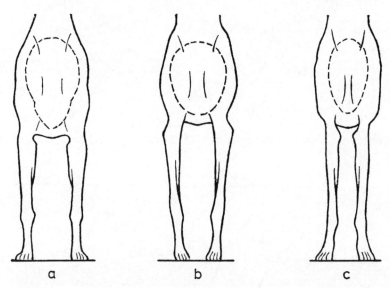

| a | b | c |

FIG. 7   Legs: (a) Correct   (b) Bow-legged   (c) 'Chippendale' legs

topline which, while sloping away a little from the shoulder to the
tail, must be in one straight line with no dip or hump, usually
referred to as saddle or roached back.

Low-set tails and stiff necks, as shown in Fig. 8(b), are invariably caused by structural faults and I shall go more deeply into
these when discussing angulation. Fig. 9 will demonstrate the
squareness of a Dobermann, although some judges do not penalise
a slightly over-long female, claiming that she needs the extra space
to carry her litters. Remembering that we have a working dog,
the ribs must be deep and reasonably well barrelled, although care
must be taken in assessing the value of this point, having in mind
that if the ribs are barrelled right to the bottom the dog will be
unable to move correctly. Fig. 7(a) shows the correct formation

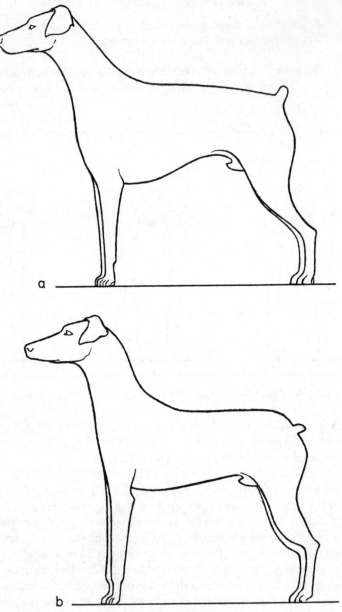

FIG. 8 (a) Ideal Dobermann (b) Faulty in structure

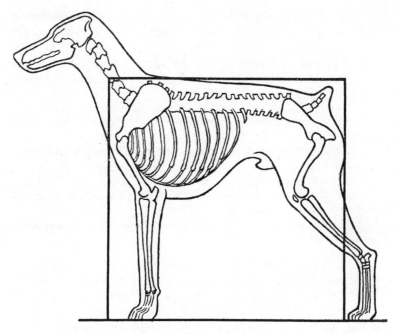

FIG. 9   Squareness

and it will be seen that the elbows are not impeded by the rib formation.

Most breeders, exhibitors and judges talk about a 'compact' Dobermann. This, of course, is really saying that the body is square, the height from ground to the highest point of the withers equalling the length from fore-chest to rear projection of the upper thigh.

However, this could be a little misleading because we could have a square Dobermann either with or without short coupling. We could also have a Dobermann with square body, but lacking in depth of brisket, which effect, in my opinion, does not give a compact appearance.

Again, we could have a specimen square in body, lacking lay-back of shoulder or having straight stifles. Such an animal is not compact, having what I term a 'boxy' look.

Maybe the best way in which to describe a compact Dobermann is to quote what was written by an American authority some ten or more years ago when he said 'A compact dog will give the impression of motion caught in an instant of suspended action and one whose ability to move will not belie the impression made when standing.'

HINDQUARTERS: Should be parallel to each other and wide enough apart to fit in with a properly built body.

The hip bone should fall away from the spinal column at an angle of about 30 degrees.

Croup well filled out.

The hindquarters should be well developed and muscular, with long bent stifle and the hocks turning neither in nor out.

While the dog is at rest, hock to heel should be perpendicular to the ground.

Here again the accent is on muscular formation, hard yet supple muscles easily visible to the eye, well developed but not cloddy, will enable the Dobermann to work all day. Do not forget the second thigh muscles which, if not developed, will give you a dog that will tire easily, proving that insufficient exercise has been given. When the dog is standing naturally, the hocks should be perpendicular to the ground, as in Fig. 9, and here particular notice should be taken of the length of the hocks. If they are too long, the dog will look unbalanced, mainly because long hocks so often go with short and straight stifles.

Occasionally, we come across over-angulated dogs which, when standing with the hocks perpendicular to the ground, have their hind feet 6 to 9 inches behind an imaginary line drawn from the end of the buttocks straight down to the ground. This gives an unbalanced appearance, and should it be a natural stance and not one exaggerated by the handler the gait will be affected. In such cases the hind legs will be continually trying to catch up with the forelegs and all rhythm of movement will be lost.

FEET: Forefeet should be well arched, compact and cat-like, turning neither in nor out.

All dew claws to be removed.

Long, flat deviating paws and weak pasterns should be penalised.

Hind feet should be well arched, compact and cat-like, turning neither in nor out.

Cat-like feet and perfectly straight legs, as shown in Figs. 8(a), 7(a) and 6 are absolute essentials, and a dog with splay feet or one sinking at the pasterns must be heavily penalised, because a Dobermann with either of these faults could not undertake the work for which it was intended.

GAIT: Should be free, balanced and vigorous with good reach in the fore-quarters, and a driving power in the hindquarters. When trotting, there should be a strong rear action drive with rotary motion of hind-quarters.
Rear and front legs should be thrown neither in nor out.
Back should remain strong and firm.

Much emphasis must be placed on correct movement, because invariably an incorrect gait means that the dog is faulty in at least one part of his body formation. Ribs barrelled right to the bottom of the brisket will cause the dog to plait, as will also badly angu-lated shoulder blades and upper arm. Weak elbows or pasterns give a peculiar paddling action, while splay feet compel the dog to flop along in a most ungainly fashion.
Cow hocks will cause weaving in the hind legs, as will also those hindquarters that are bandy or, in other words, with the feet turning inwards. The front legs should reach well forward when the dog is in motion, but with no semblance of a high-stepping action, and the hind legs, which are, after all, the driving power, should move with a bicycling movement. The whole action of a Dobermann when seen from front, rear or side must give the impression of rhythmic power.
Occasionally, we find Dobermanns with what is known as a 'pacing' action, this being similar to the gait of horses used for riding side-saddle. A pacing dog moves the two legs on the left side, followed by the two legs on the right side in unison, which gives a peculiar rolling, waddling action. This condition is easily corrected if sufficient attention is given to early training.
Much has been written and said about whether or not a Dober-mann should move on a single line or what is termed single

tracking. I have attended lectures on this subject and devoted much time to studying the movement of some of the best proportioned Dobermanns in England and the United States, and have come to the conclusion that when a correctly built Dobermann moves at a normal walk, the front and hind legs must work in parallel; as the speed is increased, and particularly when the dog is moving at a very fast pace, single tracking is automatically adopted. The speed at which we move our Dobermanns in the show ring is such that exhibits which single track are necessarily weaving both in front and at the rear, this action being caused by incorrect shoulder placement and malformed hindquarters.

TAIL: The tail should be docked at the first or second joint and should appear to be a continuation of the spine, without material drop.

A fault once prevalent in British Dobermanns, which fortunately is fast being bred out, is the falling croup or, in other words, a low-set tail. The idea is to have the tail as a continuation of the spine with no material drop, but here again this perfection is not seen often enough.

It is probably true to say that a Dobermann with a semi-erect tail or one that appears to be a straight continuation of the spine has a better temperament than the one whose tail droops from a low set position.

COAT: Should be smooth-haired, short, hard, thick and close lying. Invisible grey undercoat on neck is permissible.

Hair forming a ridge on the back of the neck and/or along the spine should be classed as a serious fault.

In my opinion the last paragraph in this section of the standard is the most important and needs clarification. Some judges have been confused with what is termed a 'cowlick' and a 'ridge'. The latter, if interpreted intelligently, can only mean a raised section of hair, whereas the former, usually a couple of inches in length, lies flat to the coat, flowing a little to the left or right instead of straight down the neck. By all means let us penalise a definite ridge that adds nothing to the beauty of a Dobermann, but let us be sensible about the cowlick, which in no way detracts from its good looks. At the time of writing this book there is a bitch carrying a cowlick who has won two challenge certificates and could soon become a champion, and I see no good reason why this should not be.

Scurf so often seen on the coat of a Dobermann is usually caused by grooming with a stiff brush. A piece of Turkish towelling is the ideal medium for grooming the dog. Occasionally, we come across a Dobermann with a longish, slightly waving coat. This is a throw-back to the Rottweiler and is undesirable.

As the shiny glistening coat on a well-bred and physically fit Dobermann is one of its most valued assets, it is valid I think if a detailed description of this asset were given. It is, of course, a single, close-lying hard-textured coat without the woolly undercoat that characterises many other breeds, and the density is such that the dog is able to withstand extremes of weather, enables it to dry out quickly, and is always clean.

Black-and-tan Dobermanns invariably carry a more dense coat than do the browns, while the blues, which are few and far between, seem to have the least dense coat. I have seen several blue-and-tan Dobermanns with very sparse coats, which most certainly detract from the overall appearance.

Browns often carry a coat that is not a uniform colour and, occasionally, yellowish patches show through. Strangely enough, this is not so obvious in the U.S.A. where there are many exhibits with deep, rich, chocolate-coloured coats.

Still thinking of colour, I am indebted to the late Philipp Gruenig for much information on this subject. Quite rightly, this expert claims that short hair is dominant over long or rough varieties, and although one or two long-haired dogs were used in the evolution of the Dobermann, cross breeding with the short-coated Manchester Terrier helped immensely to produce the lovely short coat we admire so much these days.

I understand that as far back as 1902 an experimental cross breeding to a Gordon Setter was made in Germany. This step was taken in order to improve colour and not in an attempt to lengthen the coat. The long hair of the Gordon Setter was recessive to the short hair of the Dobermann and had no effect on its length, apart from the fact that occasionally a dog will, as it grows older, develop a slightly curled coat, usually on the neck and along the back.

Other experiments in cross breeding carried out in Germany round about the early part of this century have left us with another characteristic I have referred to earlier on. This is what has become known as a ridge or cowlick and is referred to by Philipp Gruenig as a fringe, mane or bristly whirls. The ridge can occur on the muzzle, neck, or along the back, the cowlick is always confined to the neck, and the whirl invariably appears on the shoulders. I am quite convinced that all of the above characteristics can occur only if both sire and dam carry the genes to produce such results, even though they are not apparent on the dog and bitch producing the litter.

COLOUR: Colours allowed are definite Black, Brown or Blue with Rust Red markings. Markings must be sharply defined and appearing above each eye and on the muzzle, throat and fore-chest, and on all legs and feet, and below tail. White markings of any kind are highly undesirable.

It will be noticed that allowable colours are black, brown and blue and that no mention is made of what has become known as 'Isabella'. Some confusion has arisen in the United States over this rarely seen colour and at the time of writing the Dobermann Pinscher Club of America has decided to include Isabella in their Standard. From my own point of view a Dobermann of this particular colour which is rather like parchment, or old linen, should be disqualified from competition in Britain simply because it does not appear under the heading of allowable colours laid down in the British standard.

Readers will, I think, be interested to know that when I was in South Africa in 1963 I saw a litter of ten puppies about seven days old in which there were three blacks, three browns, three blues, and one Isabella. This was a truly remarkable sight and I doubt whether all four colours have ever before been born in one litter. In the United States I have seen a beautifully proportioned bitch of a colour best described as strawberry roan. Unfortunately, she was registered with the A.K.C. as an Isabella and when she is exhibited finishes either top or bottom of her class according to how the judge of the day interprets the American standard. If such a Dobermann was shown under me I would consider it a light brown and place it accordingly.

Sometimes one comes across a white patch or white hairs on the chest of Dobermann puppies and, occasionally, white feet or toe-nails can also be seen. This, of course, is a throw-back to whatever dogs were used by the original breeders during the early days of Doberdom and, fortunately, these faults are not really dominant. It has been my experience, and also that of many other breeders, that these white markings invariably disappear by the time the puppy is three months old, and never reappear.

It is interesting to note that in Germany, where breeding is strictly controlled by the German Dobermann Club, a visit to every litter is made by a responsible official to see whether there are any puppies with white markings on the chest or toes. When these are found, the breeder is told to put such puppies to sleep, otherwise no official pedigrees will be issued. Further than this, all puppies in excess of six in a litter have to be destroyed, which makes me wonder just how many potential champions are killed before being given a chance to compete in the show ring.

WEIGHT AND SIZE: Ideal height at withers: Males 27 inches. Females 25½ inches.

Considerable deviation from this ideal to be discouraged.

CHARACTER

Many things, both good and bad, have been said about the Dobermann, sometimes because of loving blindness and at other times because of ignorance. Let us try to delve into the character of this truly great breed so that those who already know Dober-manns may understand them better, and those contemplating ownership may have a better idea of what is in store for them.

Dobermann owners already know of the fanatical loyalty in-herent in the breed, which asset is visible from the moment the puppy enters your home. He loves to ride in your car, to sleep on your hearth, run in your garden, and he is playmate and guardian of your children. At least, that is what you think about it! Actually, it is you who ride in *his* car, he allows you to enjoy *his* home, he romps in *his* own garden and he plays with and protects *his* youngsters. Your only responsibility is to provide the amenities. It is this sense of ownership that endears the Dobermann to his family, making him into the best guard dog in the world, and quite candidly most humans are sufficiently egoistic to like the idea of being owned by a Dobermann.

Maybe the most dominant characteristic in our breed is alertness. His eyes, his mind, his action and appearance are all full of this quality, and what better sight is there than a top-grade Dobermann waiting to welcome you home after a day at the office or when returning from a shopping expedition.

A sense of humour is also inherent in most Dobermanns, some of them actually grinning when in a good mood, while others can give you merry hell when offering a present held firmly in the mouth, tempting you to take it and then twisting away with a terrific smile realising that you are not quick enough to handle such a supple animal.

Often I have likened a Dobermann to a thoroughbred horse, and when you see the elegance, grace, dignity, strength and balance of this breed the comparison becomes obvious.

When Dobermanns were first introduced into Britain the 'know-alls' described the dog as vicious and unsafe, and while this may be partly true of a small percentage of the breed in continental countries, it is obvious that any instability has been bred out of the modern British Dobermann. Fortunately, this has been accomplished without decreasing his strength, brain power, alertness and courage and it cannot be denied that this improvement in temperament is in the main due to imports from the U.S.A.

Most visitors to dog shows complain bitterly of the awful din set up by some exhibits, and usually it is the smaller breeds that yap like mad. How different it is on the Dobermann benches where sometimes anything up to 150 exhibits are displayed. There is little noise and what barking does take place is usually caused by provocation, and the Dobermann bark is given more as a warning than an expression of viciousness or cussedness.

It is because of his power to give warning that Dobermanns are used in some American stores as after-hours patrol dogs, and it is for the same reason they were used extensively during the war in many different parts of the world.

I know of one American store, Macy's to be precise, where about eight Dobermanns are kennelled on the roof of the building during the day and allowed to roam freely throughout the various floors during the hours of night. These dogs are trained to seek out anybody who may be hidden or moving about the store and I can imagine no less expensive type of insurance against theft.

During the war, and in particular in the Middle East, many Dobermanns were used by the Germans as message-carrying dogs, guardians of ammunition depots, and as sentry dogs. British troops who came up against these guard dogs learned to respect them, realised their qualities, and spread the gospel quite efficiently on their return to Britain.

I well remember when living at Colwood Court, in the wilds of Sussex, Club Vice-President Harry Darbyshire, then employed by the Surrey Constabulary, telephoned to say that house-breakers were operating in my district. A warning was given to me to lock away all ladders because these thieves used that method to enter houses. However, keeping a couple of adult Dobermanns in my home left my mind at ease, because previous attempts at burglary had been forestalled by my dogs.

A week or so after the warning had been given Harry Darbyshire telephoned again saying that the thieves had been apprehended and on one of then had been found a list of houses that had been, or were to be, robbed or else left severely alone. Against Colwood Court was the entry, 'Keep away, Dobermanns'.

Many publicans purchase Dobermanns as a deterrent to vandals and in almost every case reports that come back to me state that while the dog will tolerate and even be friendly with customers who remain on the correct side of the bar, he will not tolerate those who step behind.

A Dobermann is not a bully, neither does he have a mean character, but should he be attacked by another dog, or some foolhardy person, then his fighting spirit is immediately roused, usually with sad results for his opponent. He stands aloof from those outside his circle and will accept them into his home only if accompanied by one of the family, but even then will invariably keep one eye on the visitor just to make sure that nothing untoward occurs. Tremendous power is built into a Dobermann, which, together with his intelligence and skill at tracking, makes him the ideal guard and police dog.

As I have already said, many British troops who served in the Middle East during the last war returned home with stories proving the reliability, stamina and steadfastness of Dobermanns, and it is partly due to their intense enthusiasm for the breed that serious importation into England of adult stock began.

To sum up, we can claim that a Dobermann is powerful, alert, brainy and dignified. He is a devoted companion for his family and has over the years been developed for the benefit and pleasure of mankind. He is the colour of anthracite and doom, and it has been said, because of his versatility, that to own a Dobermann is to be disappointed with all other breeds.

Peggy Adamson, the well-known American breeder of Dobermanns, emphatically states that it is an 'honest' dog. Honest it certainly is, not only in character but also in conformation. There is no long coat to hide imperfections in build, no trimming is necessary to improve its appearance, and its rippling muscles remind us of a well-trained athlete.

Honesty of character is always apparent, especially when we see the loyalty and devotion given to his immediate family. He has an uncanny insight into human character, trusting those friends of the family who are readily accepted, and distrusting those who are not welcome or are strangers.

There is the true story fully reported in the national press of a male Dobermann owned by a farmer near Ely, Cambridge, which gave its life in the defence of his property. Crooks attempted to rob the house while the farmer was working his fields and the intruders who did not know of a Dobe on the property were faced with opposition. A shot was put into the dog, who continued to defend the house until several bullets killed him. Such is the great heart and loyalty inherent in the breed, and I can assure you that the above proof of devotion is not isolated, there being many

Feeding time

Sally Anne Thompson

Anne Cumbers

Puppies, aged four weeks, in the nest

C. M. Cooke

Ch. Tumlow Fantasy

Oldham Chronicl

Ch. Challenger of Sonhende

Ch. Weichardt's A-Go-Go, C.D. Ch. Iceberg of Tavey

Ch. Tumlow Winlands Flurry and Ch. Tumlow Impeccable

Ch. Acclamation of Tavey at twelve months

Sally Anne Thompson

Vanessa's Little Dictator of Tavey

storiesto demonstrate the heroism we have learned to expect from this breed.

Jean Faulks, in her chapter on Police Service, quotes other examples of the skill and courage that is inherent in the breed.

A Dobermann, however strongly built, is usually a gentle dog, allowing a baby to maul him unmercifully, while looking as though he loves the rough treatment. Neither is he the type to lick you continually, as do many other breeds; he is quite content to greet you with a welcoming smile, the wagging rear-end exhibiting as much pleasure as does the head, and then settling down with his head in your lap or pressing his body against your knee. Contact is something a Dobermann loves and is his way of expressing affection for owner and family.

To some members of the public the Dobermann is known as a vicious dog. Films and television producers, when needing to portray a 'killer dog', often use a Dobermann for that purpose, invariably selecting a black, cropped-ear male. A snarling Dobermann trained to attack is certainly a sight to deter the most hardened criminal, but so are several film actors who portray similar parts but when off the set are really docile, well-behaved humans. The Dobermann is not a killer, neither is he unreliable, and if raised in an understanding family he can be a perfect gentleman.

3

Choosing a Puppy

FOR reasons known only to yourself you are determined to buy a Dobermann puppy, and quite naturally you want the best you can afford.

If because of your needs or circumstances you feel like buying a mini car, you would think twice about visiting a Rolls-Royce agent and it is exactly the same when thinking about buying a puppy. If your tastes run to the exclusive, then call on a kennel with the reputation for producing the best, while if you require 'just a dog' there are enough people around who do not think seriously about selective breeding to help with your choice.

Dog World and *Our Dogs*, the two dog magazines that are published weekly, have Christmas annuals which are both available about the middle of December and contain reviews of many kennels that will supply the addresses you need. In addition, a letter or telephone call to the Kennel Club, 1–4 Clarges Street, Piccadilly, London W1Y 8AB (*Tel.:* 01–493–6651) will enable you to obtain the names of suitable breeders.

Maybe the best way to learn more about the selection of a suitable puppy is to visit one or more of the many championship shows, held all over Britain, where Dobermanns are exhibited. Sometimes, of course, Dobermann classes are scheduled at the smaller open shows, but at such venues the numbers exhibited are considerably less than at the larger championship shows. Have a chat with a few exhibitors who live within travelling distance of your home, find out whether they have puppies available, talk with others who appear to be successful in competition, and then make appointments to visit their kennels.

Make up your mind on the price you are willing to pay for a

puppy, knowing that the cost can range between £100 and £200 according to breeding and show propensity. Obviously, the cost of raising a good puppy is pretty high, especially when it is considered that keeping the dam, who will need extra food, vitamins and minerals during the period of gestation can, run the breeder into something approaching £200 each year. Allied to this is the money expended on a stud fee and special milk and other foods consumed by the puppy up to the date it is sold.

Remember that it is not every litter, no matter what top dogs are used as sire and dam, that produces champions at every mating, and even the most successful breeders will be able to offer companion-type dogs as well as those of show propensity. However, if you visit a breeder of repute, as distinct from what is occasionally referred to as a backyard breeder, you will have the advantage of knowing that the puppy has a better chance of being healthy and well reared, thereby probably saving the cost of repeated veterinary bills.

My next piece of advice is, take your time. When you reach the kennels, where they may have several puppies from which you can select your future companion, do not be rushed into buying the first that appeals to your eye, nor necessarily the one the breeder may say is a bargain. It is not possible to offer bargains in dogdom, because each and every puppy has a definite value according to his breeding, type, virtues and faults and, in particular, on the way in which he has been reared. As I have already said, few litters are full of potential champions and, in any case, the breeder will probably be keeping the best for himself, so state most definitely whether you require a show specimen or a pet, and whether a dog or bitch is preferred. From this information the breeder will be able to show puppies that come within your range.

Now let us look at the litter and ask ourselves the following questions. Do the dogs look masculine and the bitches feminine? Are the forelegs straight and is the bone round? Are the hindquarters firmly positioned and straight when viewed from behind? Are the eyes oval in shape and of dark colour? By now we are on the way to selecting our own puppy, so let us have a final check up and ask ourselves, is he really alert? Has he a straight topline with no material drop at the tail? Is he well balanced and

has he sufficient length of head and neck? Are his feet cat-like
with bunched knuckles? Is his coat sleek and shiny with red tan
markings?

Temperament is a feature to be carefully studied when selecting your puppy. The one that is inquisitive and comes to look you
over, the extrovert that wants to chew your shoe laces and the one
that is interested in all that is going on around him will, with
normal luck, become a show specimen of excellent temperament.

It has been proved that a dog with a gay extrovert temperament can be taught show ring behaviour better than can one with
a dull, uninspiring outlook on life. If at all possible, ask the
breeder for a sight of the sire and dam. From their temperaments
you will be able to assess with some measure of success the temperament that will eventually be acquired when your puppy
becomes mature and adult.

Now you will see why, at the beginning of this section, I advised against being hurried, and surely patience shown in selecting your companion is well worth while.

Now let us decide on the best age at which to select a puppy.
My own experience in the breed has taught that it is virtually
impossible to select the future champions before the litter reaches
four months of age. Some breeders will tell you they can pick
them from the nest. This is absolute nonsense, especially with
Dobermanns, because a newly born Dobermann with his legs
tucked up into his stomach, its mouth of a shape made expressly
for suckling and its apple-domed head, does not in any way
resemble an adult of that breed.

Certain breeders who are anxious to sell at six weeks of age will
make the mistake of selling future champions at pet prices and
vice versa. My practice is to keep the puppies until at least three or
four weeks after they have left the dam, which not only settles
them into their new way of life but enables me to attempt to sort
wheat from chaff and more truly estimate their value.

Assuming that you have selected your puppy and intend to
take it away with you, do not forget to ask the breeder for a diet
sheet, copy of pedigree, transfer form, Kennel Club Registration
Card, and ask whether or not the puppy has been treated for
worms.

It is also advisable to adhere to the breeder's diet sheet if at all possible for at least a week or so, by which time the puppy will have settled in its new home. At this stage you can gradually switch to your own ideas about feeding, possibly using the advice given in a separate chapter on this subject.

Finally, do not forget to ask whether or not the puppy has been immunised against distemper, hardpad, and hepatitis. If this has not been done, contact your vet straight away, when he will advise the best date for treatment. Do not think, should you live in an isolated spot, that your puppy cannot catch any of the above dread illnesses and that it would be a waste of money to have him immunised. I well remember in my early days of breeding and showing dogs the awful fear we all had of one of them picking up the distemper virus. Whole kennels were completely wiped out in those days, since when, thanks to research, vaccines of almost 100 per cent perfection have been produced.

In the main, this chapter has been written with the selection of a show dog in mind. There should, however, be little or no deviation from the advice given if you are seeking a companion or working dog. Why should not a working dog have the same physical attributes as one that can enter breed competitions and why should a companion dog be totally inferior? Many owners of Dobermanns have dogs that compete successfully in beauty competitions and also acquire qualifications in working tests. Such dogs are good companions to their owners, not only pleasing to the eye and able to guard and protect the family but also able to give the love and affection that makes this breed so attractive.

THE NEW PUPPY IN YOUR HOME

There are few things in this world as appealing, and with such complete charm, as a new puppy of any breed. Your Dobermann puppy, with soft eyes, plump belly and oversized legs and feet, will win your heart with your first look. The almost irresistible temptation to rush to him, pick him up in your arms and just cuddle the life out of him is all wrong. No matter what his age, whether he be eight weeks or four months, restraint must be used.

Rule No. 1 with a new puppy is to let him find out about you before you worry too much about finding out about him. Let him wander around and find all the new smells; he will be as excited as you are, but leave him alone and also keep calm yourself. Eventually he will come to you. Let him do the sniffing around; he will quickly associate what his nose tells him: that you are more or less the boss. When he has come to you and sniffed his fill, pat him gently and scratch behind his ears, then ignore him.

You will, of course, know from his breeder what his diet and routine have been. Don't try to change this overnight because he will be excited and enough of a problem to you without getting his digestion upset. It is probable that in missing his litter mates he will even go without food for a day or two, and provided he is not running a temperature you should not be unduly worried. The old maxim that a dog will eat when hungry still holds true and in a few days' time you should be able to switch your puppy to your own ideas of diet, maybe using the chart shown at the end of this chapter.

It must be remembered that this feeding chart is given only as a guide and it must also be remembered that every dog is an individual and variations will be necessary according to appetite, especially as he grows on, and according to the owner's particular time-table and habits.

Let me emphasise here that it is essential your puppy receives a good intake of calcium, best given by way of milk, bone flour, calcium lactate, Vivomin or similar preparation, especially during the time when the second teeth are coming through. It is also essential that halibut oil or cod-liver oil be given at the same time because this helps the body more easily to absorb the calcium instead of allowing most of it to pass right through the stomach and intestines. It must also be remembered that teeth are mainly composed of calcium and that the bone structure of a puppy will suffer should insufficient calcium be given at this critical period. Another good idea, if it is your wish to see good solid bone and perfectly formed white teeth, is to ask your veterinary surgeon to give an injection of Nandrolin when the puppy is between three and four months of age.

It is certainly wise to imagine that having a new puppy in your home is rather like having a new baby: watchfulness and anticipation are the key words to your and his success.

Soon you will have become acquainted and you are ready to feed him properly. You have already bought his bed and decided on the place where it is to stand. The puppy must quickly be taught to know that this is his rightful place and that it is his refuge and his sanctuary. This can be done by putting him on the bed and talking softly to him as you pet him. After a few times of doing this he will begin to relax on his bed and will stay there for even a couple of minutes after you have left the area which, in effect, means that the battle is in the process of being won.

The next important thing is to teach him that his bed is the place where he is expected to sleep, and here I must give strong warning that you do not give way to impulse to let him sleep on the foot of your bed. Every puppy has a wonderfully retentive mind and there is a lot of difference between a 15 lb puppy at the foot of your bed and a 90 lb adult Dobermann who has learnt that the bed really belongs to him and, although he is willing to share it with you, quietly expands to take up considerably more than his half. I know of one lady enthusiast in this breed who made this mistake; the puppy looked so sweet at the foot of the single bed that he was allowed to sleep there from the day first purchased. Last time I spoke to her she had just spent a considerable sum of money on an over-sized double bed.

Incidentally, it is a good idea when teaching a puppy exactly where he is expected to sleep to put an old glove or sock in his bed. This gives him the idea that he has not completely lost contact with his new owners, and in all probability the puppy will fall asleep dreaming of the nice people who had the good sense to acquire him.

On the subject of sleep, I must make a similar comparison as used in a previous paragraph. All mothers know that a baby needs as much sleep as it is possible to have, and it is as true with puppies as it is with babies that while sleeping they grow on, and their temperaments improve. Not only this, but it is much more comfortable for the owner to have his puppy asleep for much of the day than having him under his feet.

Another word of warning to those new owners who have young children around the house. Impress upon them that when the puppy is asleep he should be left on his bed and not awakened in order to romp and play. Forbid the children to pick the puppy up by his legs because this can cause irreparable damage. If the puppy has to be picked up for any reason whatsoever, it is best to put one hand under his belly and the other just between the forelegs. In this way the puppy will feel perfectly safe and there is no risk of damage to his elbows and shoulders.

For some strange reason babies and puppies have to eliminate more frequently than statisticians can compute. The necessity for relief seems almost constant, so perhaps the following couple of rules will help you housebreak your puppy.

First of all, take him outside to a regular place first thing in the morning and last thing before you go to bed at night. Also, take him outside to the regular place immediately after he wakes from a sleep and as soon as he has finished a meal. Directly he has relieved himself, tell him he is a 'fine fellow', give him a pat on the shoulders and quickly he will learn that outdoors is the place for certain jobs. Be prepared, of course, for the time he soils the carpet, when a gentle scolding, never a hard cuff given in the heat of temper, followed by being put outside to finish the misdemeanour, should soon teach him the error of his ways.

In my own home it is a golden rule never to smack a dog on the rear because this is inclined to make him suspicious of people behind. We have found it helps, when a crime of sufficient gravity warrants corporal punishment, to take the puppy by the loose skin under the neck and shake his head with reasonable force while cussing like mad. Incidentally, this helps to relieve one's own temper. This treatment hurts his pride far more than it does his body and fixes the crime more firmly in his mind. Always remember to praise him when he does the correct thing and to remonstrate when he errs. This is an essential principle of all training, whether it be teaching him where to sleep, house-breaking or lead training. Use the same words every time you praise your Dobermann puppy, such as 'good boy', and try to use the same tone of voice. It is the inflection as much as the words that will help him to understand that you are praising him when he does well or correcting him when he has misbehaved. A pat when he is good and a severe shaking of his head when he is bad, given at the same time as you speak to him, emphasise the words and impress them in his mind, but remember to be as liberal with your praises as you are with your criticisms. Never strike your puppy in anger and do not let punishment for him come out of your bad temper; always be calm, temperate and swift. The praise or the punishment must immediately follow the act. Your Dobermann is far too busy mentally and physically to be able to associate either a kind word and a pat or a harsh word and a spank with an action which has already passed. If you have missed the act itself, forget all about it.

Now we are ready to teach him one of the first necessities for the well-mannered and gentlemanly Dobermann, which is how to behave himself on a lead. Lead breaking should begin just as soon as you are acquainted with each other. It is the essential point upon which his other acts of obedience will be taught. In my own kennels we use a simple choke chain collar which is a link chain about 4 inches longer than the circumference of the Dobermann's neck, with solid rings at both ends. The method of using this choke collar is to hold one ring and drop the chain through, put it over the puppy's head so that the draw is across the back of the neck with the ring attached to your lead, passed through the stationary ring from his left shoulder toward his right shoulder. You must be particularly careful in making the collar from this simple length of chain because if used incorrectly the collar will become a choke at all times instead of falling loose when the dog is walking properly at heel. The lead itself should be quite supple, made of leather and about 4 feet in length.

Let us assume you have assembled the collar and lead and placed it over the puppy's head; believe me, you are now about to have quite a time for the next few minutes. The puppy is not going to like this restraint at all. Patience and calmness are very necessary. Try to keep the puppy calm as well, otherwise you will soon be in the position of playing him like a fish when he lunges away in an effort to free himself from this unknown thing around his neck. Sooner or later he will sit fairly quietly with you at his side, especially if you speak quietly and lovingly to him. Never attempt a tug of war with your puppy; always use short, sharp jerks on the lead. Remember what happened the first time you attempted to pull or push the fellow with whom you played at school; he just pulled or pushed back. Remember also the time you administered a short sharp push to the same fellow. You jerked him to his senses. If your puppy runs ahead, turn completely round with hardly a stop, at the same time giving a jerk and saying 'Heel', and after four or five treatments such as this he will keep by your side. This is the moment to stop and give a lot of praise to the puppy.

I cannot emphasise too greatly the need to lead train your puppy correctly because there is nothing worse than to see an adult Dobermann taking his owner for a walk. Not only is it extremely tiring to the arm muscles, but the sight of a fully grown dog pulling its owner along the street is bad for the reputation of any breed and makes life miserable for both dog and owner.

A correctly trained dog should walk evenly at heel, with his head roughly at the left-hand knee of the owner, so that the choke chain hangs loosely around the neck, thus making life comfortable for both. Bear in mind that one day your Dobermann may appear in breed competition and that if your dog walks freely with you when asked to move to and fro across the ring, the judge has a much better chance of assessing gait, etc.

FEEDING CHART

12 weeks of age: 4 meals daily

8.00 a.m.	½-pint of Milk mixed with one raw egg, 1 dessertspoon Glucose and 2 dessertspoons Farex.
12.00	6 oz raw minced meat, thoroughly mixed with one large handful of Puppy Meal which has been soaked in gravy. Add 1 teaspoon Stress and 2 Halibut Oil Capsules. NOTE: The mixture must not be sloppy.
4.00 p.m.	Repeat the 8.00 a.m. meal, omitting the egg.
8.00 p.m.	Repeat the midday meal.

Increase the daily meat content by 1 ounce each fortnight.

20 weeks of age: 3 meals daily

8.00 a.m.   8 oz raw minced meat, thoroughly mixed with one large
              handful of Puppy Meal which has been soaked in gravy.
              Add one teaspoon Stress and 2 Halibut Oil Capsules.

2.00 p.m.   ½ pint of Milk mixed with one raw egg and 1 dessert-
              spoon Glucose and 2 dessertspoons Farex.

8.00 p.m.   Repeat the 8.00 a.m. meal.

Increase the daily meat content by 2 ounces each fortnight.

6 months of age: 2 meals daily

8.00 a.m.   12 oz raw minced meat, thoroughly mixed with two
              large handfuls Terrier Meal soaked in gravy. Add 1
              teaspoon Stress and 2 Halibut Oil Capsules.

Midday   Give half dozen Milkwheat Biscuits.

6.00 p.m.   Repeat the 8.00 a.m. meal and add one raw egg.

12 months of age: 1 meal daily

8.00 a.m.   Give half dozen Milkwheat Biscuits.

6.00 p.m.   1¼ to 1½ lb raw minced meat, thoroughly mixed with
              two large handfuls of Terrier Meal soaked in gravy.
              Add one dessertspoon of Stress and 2 Halibut Oil
              Capsules or 1 teaspoon Codliver Oil.

*From the very beginning give your puppy 8 Vetzyme Tablets every day. Usually
the dog will take these from your hand.*

4

Management and Feeding

I SUPPOSE that the management and feeding of dogs has been dealt with hundreds of times by hundreds of breeders, many of whom differ widely in their experience and ideas. However, we have a happy, well-contented and healthy lot of Dobermanns so perhaps my thoughts on how best to house dogs could be of interest.

A dog that is kept outdoors for most of the day treats his kennel as his home and refuge and his run as a garden in which part of his daily exercise can be taken. This run or garden should help him keep healthy and fit and it should have a surface that can be easily kept clean and hygienic. The run or exercising paddock should be of cement, which will help to keep his feet tight and cat-like and at the same time keep toenails short. It has been proved beyond doubt that a dog that moves all the time on grass and that has insufficient exercise on hard roads, develops splayed feet. Poor feet can, of course, be a trait inherited from the sire or dam, in which case no amount of moving on cement runs or hard roads will correct it. Assuming that the parents have good tight feet and that the puppy is correctly fed, exercised and raised, a cement run can do no harm and must be of benefit.

A grass area cannot be as easily cleaned down as can a surface of cement, and many of the diseases and illnesses that beset dogs are caused by urine and faeces that cannot adequately be disposed of if left to lie around on grass or similar absorbent surfaces. Incidentally, the cement should be slightly rough, not smooth, because snow or icy conditions can make a cement surface very slippery.

Since, however, a cement surface can become quite hot in summer, it is advisable to use a wooden platform, height about

3 inches and approximately 4 feet square, on which several puppies or a couple of adults can rest to bask in the sun. These wooden platforms are also a great asset after rainfall because they dry out much more quickly than does cement or any other surface.

It is a pleasing sight to see a litter of Dobermann puppies all in a bunch lying asleep on these wooden benches which, no matter what the weather is, they seem to prefer to the concreted ground. The benches should not be painted or covered with linoleum or anything similar because puppies while teething will in all probability chew at the wood and possibly swallow paint or pieces of non-digestible material which can do them harm. For some unknown reason, maybe because of boredom, Dobermann puppies like to eat stones, and several years ago when we allowed youngsters in our own kennel to run loose on grass, we found they took a great delight in digging into the soil, finding stones or pebbles, and then swallowing them. In most cases the odd stone or two passes easily through the puppy's stomach and has no bad effect but experience has shown that, occasionally, several stones can be swallowed and can lodge in the intestines. This, if found out in time, necessitates an immediate operation and if the condition is neglected, a dead puppy is the result. It is therefore obvious for many reasons such as hygiene, cleanliness, conditioning and safety that a cement run supersedes all others.

As for the kennel in which the dog will spend most of the day and possibly all of the night, we favour wooden buildings with exterior surfaces faced with sheet asbestos. Fortunately, in Britain there are many manufacturers of inexpensive sectional wooden kennels that any handyman can easily erect, and it is a simple matter to buy sheet asbestos from a local builder or builder's merchant, cut it to size, and then cover the various sections of the kennel. Wooden beading about 1 inch wide should be used along each edge of the asbestos when nailing it to the kennel.

Asbestos keeps the kennel cool in summer and warm in winter and, what is equally important, prevents the wood from rotting and eliminates continual repainting. Our kennels are lined with hardboard, which is easily cleaned and therefore free from germs, etc., and the interior of the roof is lined with expanded polystyrene which helps keep the occupants warm during the winter.

All this may appear to be expensive but as it eliminates the necessity of repainting and keeps the dogs warm and happy, it is in the long run cheaper than just a plain wooden kennel. Incidentally, it is our practice to leave the main kennel door open day and night, partially closing it by means of a 12 inch-long hook and staple. This practice is adopted even throughout the winter so that the dogs can leave their kennel at any time to relieve themselves away from their bedding. Puppies, of course, need a little more coddling than do adults, so we place a small square box within the kennel with its aperture facing away from the main door. In this way puppies are not exposed to draughts or cold winds and will cuddle down, together, setting up their own heating system.

Now consider the various forms of bedding that are used in kennels. In my opinion, straw is dangerous, not only because it can harbour fleas but because the sharp ends can easily pierce a puppy's eyes. The old blanket can satisfactorily be used, although some puppies, especially when going through the teething stage, may be inclined to chew at the ends, and I can think of nothing more indigestible than wool. Newspaper is cheap and easily disposed of when soiled, but this gives little comfort on cold nights. We use wood wool, which is quite easily obtainable, gives warmth and safety, and burns quite readily when the bedding is changed once or twice each week. Incidentally, sawdust, although an asset in the puppies' runs, should not be used in the actual bed, because deep breathing while the Dobermann sleeps can lead to absorption through the nostrils.

Now for the walls of the run. Quite recently we came across a material known as corrugated Polystyrene. It is inexpensive and can be obtained opaque or in several colours and makes an ideal wall when fitted to the inside of the chain-link fencing. It is clean, can be hosed down easily, and puppies in particular cannot catch their feet when leaping up to greet a visitor, as is the case with chain-link fencing. What is also important is that the dogs seem to be quieter when partially concealed behind opaque walls, and this is particularly useful when living in a crowded area.

Most of the above has been written from my own experience as an owner of a reasonably large establishment where the majority of dogs are kennelled outside. There are, however, many 'one-dog' owners who may be entering dogdom for the first time or about to enjoy the experience of possessing their first ever Dobermann. I know of several flat-dwellers living in large towns who enjoy the companionship of their Dobermann. It is a fallacy to think that a dog of this size cannot exist comfortably in a flat, although it must be admitted that a mixture of living outdoors during the day and in the house at night is preferable.

Anyhow, let us consider the flat-dweller first of all. A Dobermann is one of the cleanest dogs in existence and is easily house trained. It is essential that his education in house training begins as soon as he enters his new home, a subject that has been dealt with in Chapter 3. Regular exercise is essential, especially after the puppy has reached the age of five to six months. This should not be overdone at any time during his lifetime, and walks, preferably on a hard surface, of twenty to thirty minutes twice a day should be sufficient. Should you live near a park or common-land, and after you are confident that the dog will return to you when called, a ten-minute romp, even in grass, will do no harm and help take some of the steam out of him.

Regular visits to a local training school will help both you and the dog to learn exactly what is meant by obedience training, and after the lessons have been absorbed both you and he will live a more orderly life.

Earlier, I suggested that a Dobermann should not be allowed to sleep on your bed, and now that I repeat this advice, we must consider where and how he is to sleep. It will soon be found that your dog will adopt his own armchair, so if you do not object to this, then let it be his refuge and bed from then on. Should you resent such treatment to your furniture, a wooden box approximately 3 feet square with walls about 12 inches high should be provided. This can be lined with a blanket or rug and the box should stand a few inches off the ground. Most flats and houses these days are well heated, so make sure there is always a bowl of clean water strategically placed so that your dog can slake his thirst.

The owner who has a garden, however, and intends that his dog shall live outside part of the day would be well advised to fence off a section as large as can be spared, surround it by chain-link fencing 5 to 6 feet high and, if possible, cover the surface with concrete. On this surface should be placed a wooden plat-form, as already described, and a wooden kennel approximately 4 ft by 3 ft which could be his refuge when it rains or when the sun shines strongly. Keep in mind that a bowl of clean water must also be provided in the run and make sure that it is emptied and cleaned daily. This is absolutely essential, especially if you live in a district where rats can enter the run, because they may con-taminate the water and the dog will most surely contract hepatitis.

FEEDING

Having dealt with the feeding of puppies in the previous chapter, we should now consider how best to nurture an adult. As is well known, food is, because of its chemical content, essential to all living creatures, and it is of course the quality of food that will determine the degree of fitness and well-being in any animal.

A dog is naturally carnivorous and therefore needs meat, and while I know that some breeders, and in particular owners of boarding kennels, feed tripe, offal, and the like to their inmates, and while I agree that most boarders enter the kennel in a condi-tion that a sparse diet over the space of a couple of weeks will do them little or no harm, I am confident that good raw meat is an essential towards building the sleek, shiny, muscular Dobermann we all admire so much.

Bulk in the form of biscuit meal is, of course, necessary because the protein in meat needs such an additive to round off the diet and the body of the dog. It is our habit in the Tavey kennels to introduce yeast tablets at each meal, plus, especially in the winter months, either halibut oil capsules or cod liver oil.

Many breeders add various vitamin compounds and bone meal to the diet of their dogs and this depends on the individual and veterinary advice. It is undoubtedly true that according to whether we use suitable or inadequate foods so we shall produce a dog of either healthy, well-developed and muscular type or an unfit, meagre and sickly animal.

While thinking of good or bad feeding having a great influence on the welfare and fitness of a dog, I would like to digress a little and touch on the subject of hygiene. All the best feeding in the world will not produce a strong dog unless it lives in clean conditions. I know of several kennels which after years of use have become what could be termed 'dog sour'. This is caused by repeated urination and droppings being left on the ground, thus encouraging bacteria to form with the result that the inmates eventually suffer. The only way to combat this trouble is to make absolutely sure that all filth is cleared away at least twice a day and to use a flame gun or lime to burn the ground at least once a year, thereby removing most forms of germs and bacteria.

Now back to feeding. While all the comments made above are generally true, it must be remembered that a dog is not a machine into which when certain foods are fed, definite results will be obtained. Each dog is an individual, some preferring raw to cooked meat, others refusing a dish when it contains cod liver oil, and some abhorring fish, while their kennel mates enjoy it whether cooked or dried. It is up to the owner by trial and error to find out what is preferred by his dog and then to pander to such idiosyncrasies that will help the dog both bodily and mentally.

It is well to remember that, as the dog grows older, overfeeding, thereby causing a fat condition, can do nothing but shorten the animal's life. Of course, the same applies to underfeeding because prolonged undernourishment will cause mental distress followed by sickness and death. It is up to the owner to make sure that adequate, but not too much, food is given and the best guide is to watch the bodily condition and suppleness of the animal, bearing in mind that a Dobermann will eat and need more food in winter than in summer.

Stud dogs need rather different feeding from brood bitches, the former requiring just as much protein as will keep them in good hard condition. Naturally the same applies to brood bitches when not in whelp, but directly after mating special and more detailed care must be taken (*see* Chapter 5).

Finally, it must be realised that good feeding and good breeding go together and it is because, fortunately, we have several breeders in England who realise this fact that the quality of Dobermanns in the island is so high.

EXERCISE

I suppose we have all seen the owner who attaches his dog to a long lead and then takes the animal for a trot, often for several miles, trailing along beside his bicycle. This, in my opinion, can do nothing beyond tiring the dog unnecessarily and using up calories that are best conserved in its body. Other owners insist that a Dobermann needs a couple of hours' sharp walk each and every day which, although it may be good for the owner's waist-line, produces no better results as regards conditioning the animal than does the system adopted in the Tavey kennels.

Our dogs are allowed five to ten minutes' free exercise in a large grass paddock, where running freely they should soon get rid of steam and expend much energy. The dogs are then taken for a twenty-minute slow walk along a hard-surfaced lane and it is this type of exercise that keeps their body in show condition and their nails of correct length.

Readers will notice that I write of a slow walk, and by this I really mean slow, not fast. It is surely obvious that when a dog is moving at a trot or a very fast pace he has impetus of motion which means that he is not carrying his full weight. If he travels slowly, preferably uphill, he must thrust with his hindquarters and pull a little with his forequarters, t hus causing all muscles to be used to the utmost advantage. In this way his thighs, and in particular the second thighs, will develop, the muscles under the armpits will also tighten, thereby holding the elbows correctly in position and, provided it is inborn, the feet will remain cat-like.

At this stage I would warn owners that too much exercise on grass or soft ground with little movement on a hard surface will surely cause the feet to spread or splay, which is ugly and a bad fault in the show ring.

Of course, if your Dobermann lives in a built-up area where little or no grass is available it will be necessary to exercise him on the pavement for a longer time than twenty minutes each day. However, I repeat that miles and miles of exercising will not condition him any better than a half hour's slow walk, especially if the weather is wet and cold, which is hated just as much by the dog as it is by the owner.

5

Breeding and Puppy-rearing

WHETHER you have bought a Dobermann bitch of royal pedigree
who grows on to be a champion or you have purchased a companion-type female the day will come when you will consider
breeding a litter, even if only to have the pleasure of seeing half
a dozen or so tiny mites for whose welfare and upbringing you
will be responsible. There is nothing so beautiful, unless it be
your own baby, as a litter of dogs eagerly feeding at the dam and
then rolling over to sleep it off. There is nothing so satisfying as
watching the love and care given to a healthy litter by the mother
and nothing pleases your own ego more than watching the
puppies open their eyes, then wobble about on unsteady legs, and
finally realising that it was your devoted attention that helped
form them into solid, brave and attractive Dobermanns.

It may be unnecessary to point out that great care must be
exercised when selecting the sire of your future litter, nevertheless
I must repeat again and again that only the best is good enough.
By this I do not necessarily mean that the top winning dog of the
day must automatically be used; it is far better to select a sire who,
mated to a bitch of similar breeding to your own, has produced
first-class specimens. This may mean that several journeys to
dog shows have to be made but such expenditure of time and
money will produce the best results.

Indiscriminate breeding I abhor, too much of it is practised in
Britain today, and I suggest that the subject is approached in the
manner adopted by the Germans and the Americans who study
blood lines, type and temperament to a degree some of us in
Britain could well copy. Of course, the top breeding kennels in
Britain do pay attention to selective breeding and it is doubtless

for that reason we now produce a few Dobermanns that could compete anywhere in the world. My remarks are really intended for the one-bitch owner who so often, when deciding to breed a litter, thinks only of 'the dog round the corner'. Planning a mating should not be left until your bitch first comes into season because this leaves insufficient time to study the subject and to write around for copies of pedigrees or stud cards.

Another point to keep in mind is the economics of producing and eventually selling puppies. Stud fees for Dobermanns range between £40 and £100, the former usually for unknown dogs and the latter for those who have won well in the show ring and who have proved their dominance as sires. Assuming that a litter of five is born and a cheap stud fee has been paid, it will easily be seen that the average cost is £8 per puppy, but if a better dog has been used at a fee of say £60, the average cost is £12.

It is quite difficult to sell Dobermann puppies at anything above £20 to £30 when the sire is unknown, whereas often, with the help of the stud dog's owners, figures of £125 to £200 are obtainable. It does not need a slide rule or an A Level in mathematics to realise the wisdom of using the best dog available and, after all, it costs just as much to raise mediocre puppies as it does to raise those of good type.

A further point to bear in mind is that should, for any reason at all, your bitch not conceive, the more reputable breeder will, as an act of courtesy, usually offer a repeat mating free of charge. It must, however, be fully understood that there is no definite obligation on the stud-dog owner to offer the repeat service, the fee paid being simply for using the dog at stud and is not dependent on the production of a litter. In certain cases arrangements can be made that instead of paying a fee for the stud dog, pick of litter may be taken. Should this method be adopted, it is best that an exchange of letters, which could be interpreted as a contract, be made between the owners of both dog and bitch.

Now let us look at the procedure of arranging a mating for your bitch, having already decided on the stud dog to be used, and having received confirmation from the owner that the dog will be available. Directly the bitch first shows colour and the vulva begins to swell, advice should be sent to the stud dog owner who, being an expert, will suggest the best day for the visit. This is usually twelve or thirteen days after the season begins, so great care must be exercised to make sure of the date when colour is first seen.

And so we arrive at the day on which you take the bitch to the dog. On arrival, ask permission from the owner for your bitch to relieve herself at some convenient spot, preferably away from the mating precincts so that the stud has no other distraction apart from the bitch herself. Some breeders prefer to allow dog and bitch to have a little flirtation prior to mating and this is all very well if the latter is completely ready to accept the former. Often this is not quite the case and can result in the dog being bitten and frightened, which could put him off stud work for the rest of his life. In my own kennels we make a practice of muzzling the bitch by tying a figure of eight bandage around the muzzle and neck, adding a leather collar which, when held by the owner or an assistant, enables the bitch to be controlled while a second person directs the dog correctly after he has mounted his mate. Such a procedure instils confidence in the stud, which quickly realises that he cannot be bitten and gets the work over and finished in good time. When the tie is effected, you will have what seems to be an endless wait of approximately 30 minutes, while the sperm is entering the uterus and it is at this time you and the owner can sit back, have a cigarette and discuss the future champions to be born in 63 days' time. This is also the moment when you both hope with all your heart that the ova have descended into the fallopian tubes. Incidentally, it is not absolutely essential that a tie takes place after copulation and it is our practice at the Tavey kennels to hold the dog in position when ejaculation has taken place for at least two minutes prior to turning his front legs over the bitch.

I well remember assisting in an experiment some few years ago when Mr. Harrap, the celebrated veterinary surgeon at the Royal College of Veterinary Surgeons in London, demonstrated that the first minute of ejaculation contained little or no sperm and that almost 100 per cent was given during the second minute. The remaining period of the tie was taken up by the extrusion of liquid almost free from sperm and by the bitch's contractions encouraging it to travel further up the fallopian tubes. There are literally many thousands of spermatozoa that enter the uterus and it is only a minute proportion that connect with the eggs within the bitch, thus causing conception.

Some four weeks after mating it is possible to feel tiny hard lumps when pressing the bitch's belly and some breeders will claim that the size of the litter can be foretold at this time. However, we do not probe around the underside of a bitch in whelp, lest such rough treatment could damage the embryo puppies. It is just as well to exercise a little patience and wait until the sixth week after mating, when obvious signs will show whether or not the bitch is in whelp.

Now for a few warnings, especially if it is your wish not to mate your bitch. Rest assured that neighbours' dogs will know even before you do when the bitch is about to start her season. It is probable that her urine carries a particular odour just before and during season and you know as well as I do what odours can do to a male dog of good or average scenting powers. Available at chemists there are several medicaments that will help counteract the odour, but it must be remembered that they do not destroy every smell. The bitch must during the period of her season be exercised on a lead, and if this is not practicable she should be placed in a recognised and efficient boarding kennel until all is clear. There are also special panties available at good dog shops for use during this period and they are invaluable if you live outside town where your bitch is normally allowed freedom.

Another point to keep in mind is that in all probability your bitch will experience her first season at about nine months of age but as this, in my opinion, is far too young for any dog to be mated, you should curb your impatience for a little and not breed from her until she is fifteen months old at the earliest. Few Dobermanns are really matured, and this applies also to the male, until they reach the age of fifteen months, and it is surely better to produce a litter from an adult bitch than from one which at the age of nine months is still very much a juvenile.

Thinking back on my comments on the selection of a stud, and realising that this chapter is mainly devoted to those who have their first-ever Dobermann, I would strongly suggest, assuming the bitch is a maiden, or virgin, that a dog with past experience of mating be used. Young dogs, especially those who have not previously had a bitch, can be a little diffident when first offered a mating, and much time and effort can be lost while both are making up their minds with regard to procreation.

Now to consider how to handle the male while mating is being prepared and put into operation. I have covered part of this subject when discussing the female, but it will do no harm to mention that first and foremost your dog must be fit and that, even though extremely popular with owners of bitches, some restriction must be put on the amount of work he is to undertake. Of course, dogs vary in virility and strength but, generally speaking, twice a week with a good long rest after a month's work is quite sufficient for a strong, masculine and potent stud.

Some folk will tell you that certain dogs produce a predominance of males while others are well known to sire a preponderance of females. According to my experience, this is absolute nonsense, since only half a dozen or so out of the thousands of sperm injected into the bitch cause conception. I am more inclined to believe the theory that if a bitch is mated early in her season, she is likely to produce more of her own sex, because nature assumes that an early mating in the natural state implies that there are more males available than there are females. It could also be true that if a bitch is mated late in her season, she will give birth to more males than females because nature assumes a shortage of males.

Earlier I mentioned the advisability of using an experienced dog on a virgin bitch and the reverse is the case with a young stud dog. I know full well that an inexperienced male will take a devil of a time fooling around, being not too certain of what is expected of him unless a bitch who has had previous litters is there to encourage him. Here I would reiterate my advice that even if a bitch is experienced and ready and willing to stand, that she be muzzled and held firmly because this will give the stud dog confidence. In my own kennels we keep a special bandage and a thick leather collar for this work and it is fact that my stud dogs, directly they see the bandage and collar, know what is expected of them.

Do please remember that four weeks after your bitch has been mated, her embryo puppies will start to take something from her constitution. This is the time to increase the food intake slowly, keeping in mind that a dog's stomach does not enlarge as the puppies develop and therefore cannot take overlarge doses of food. It is best to divide her feeds into twice each day, say at 10 a.m. and 4 p.m., thus enabling her to take her fill and digest the first meal before the second is given.

And so we come to the raising of a litter, the worries, strains and delights of which are dealt with in a separate chapter. It must, however, be realised that Dobermanns cannot be bred for profit; the cost of keeping a bitch, the stud fee for the dog, and expenditure in the way of feeding, the veterinary surgeon's bills, immunisation etc. running away with most of what you may obtain for the litter. Satisfaction you certainly will have, and a sense of having achieved something you will enjoy, but if your outgoings almost cover your receipts, you will be a fortunate person.

It is this continual striving for perfection that makes dog breeding one of the most rewarding hobbies in the world and I know full well that if you do not produce a champion in your first litter, you will continue to produce others until the thrill of owning and having bred a top specimen is achieved.

Incidentally, do not think, when your puppies are almost ten weeks old, that all of your 'geese are swans'. This rarely happens and it is more than likely you have reached a good average instead of a litter of champions. This is the moment to take stock and to be really critical of the results. Nothing is worse than the breeder suffering from kennel blindness because this can only lead to disappointment. Check your puppies to see whether all, or almost all, carry the same faults or virtues. Be honest with yourself about this, even if it means that your choice of sire was incorrect or even if your bitch is not of a quality that will assist in improving the breed. If the former is the case, try a different stud next time, and if you feel that your bitch is greatly to blame, then do not breed from her again. Should the results be good or outstanding, you can do nothing better than repeat the mating when next your bitch is in season.

It is usually found that line breeding from good stock will give far better results than indiscriminate breeding and I like very much the system of mating the best grand-daughter to her grandfather or the best grandson to his grandmother. This, I understand, is the system used extensively by breeders of Arab horses and when we consider the very definite head type, body conformation and gait of this lovely breed, it is, in my opinion, proven that the system is correct.

So far in this chapter I have dealt in the main with the females but the stud dog has an equal part in determining the type of puppies to be produced. The stud must be fit and virile, otherwise the results can be very disappointing. I have heard of owners of bitches, often travelling quite a distance for a mating to be effected, refusing a service because the male is underweight, dirty and obviously out of condition. If you own a dog that is put to public stud, it is your responsibility to see that he is fit and in a condition to receive a mate.

WHELPING

Many breeders will state emphatically that in order to maintain the good health of a bitch, she should be allowed to have one or more litters. I am in agreement with this theory because, after all, nature has given her the organs and bodily system to act as a mother, and experience has proved that temperament in particular can be impaired if a bitch never has puppies, whereas the one who has been allowed to perform this natural function lives a more contented life.

Let us assume that you wish to breed a litter and the sire of your future puppies has been selected. Maybe the first decision you must make when planning the whelping of your bitch is whether she will have the litter outdoors or in the house. Should you have decided to whelp her inside your home you will need to provide a whelping box only, but if she is to have her puppies out of doors, a draught-proof kennel or shed in addition to the box must be purchased.

It is advisable that the bitch should become used to living and

sleeping in this new environment, so introduce her to the whelping box and encourage her to occupy it several days before the
litter is due.

Over the centre of the box, suspended approximately 3 feet
from the base, should be an infra-red lamp of the dull emitter
type. The purpose of this lamp is not solely to provide a gentle
comforting heat but is also intended to help dry each puppy after
it is born and while the dam is giving birth to and tending the
puppies that follow. Further than this, it will be found that a few
days after the litter has arrived, the puppies will quietly curl up
in a heap under the beneficial rays of the lamp, allowing the bitch
to leave them in comfort while occasionally resting outside the
whelping box.

The shed or kennel should be of sufficient size for the puppies
to frolic when up on their feet at the age of three or four weeks
and of sufficient height to enable you to move around in comfortably when cleaning away the debris, of which there will be plenty
during the several weeks after birth.

The whelping box must, of course, be placed well away from
the door of the shed so that draughts caused when the door is
opened does not affect the dam or the puppies. Layers of clean
newspaper are ideal as a bedding for the box and in my opinion
are far superior and more hygienic than straw or sawdust, both of
which are used by some breeders. Newspaper is quickly and easily
changed after the puppies are born and more particularly during
the next four or five weeks when the bed will be continually soiled.
Another advantage of using newspaper is that it is more easily
burned, thus contributing to hygienic conditions.

An ideal whelping box for Dobermanns should stand 3 inches
off the floor and be approximately 4 ft × 4 ft with a pig rail
around three sides extending about 3 inches, and placed at a
height of 5 inches. This will allow a puppy to take refuge if it
wants to, and also prevent the bitch from crushing the litter
against the walls. The fourth side of the whelping box should
be hinged with narrow slats running across the width and fitted
with small staples and hooks so that it can make a four-sided
closed box for use while the puppies are unable to walk. These
slats will enable the puppies more easily to climb back into the

bed when eventually they are up on their feet and after they have been running around the kennel or kitchen.

Dobermanns usually whelp their litters quite easily so, assuming that the bitch has become used to sleeping in the box lined with layers of newspaper, and that the infra-red lamp, which should have been switched on a couple of days before, is functioning correctly, all is ready for the great event.

I know that many breeders adopt the practice of worming an in-whelp bitch soon after mating has taken place. Although we do not favour this system in my own kennels, there is no harm done if a good worming liquid or pills recommended by your vet is used because it will in no way affect the embryo litter, but will remove any worms that may exist in the bitch.

During the first half of the nine weeks gestation period, the bitch should be allowed to lead her normal life with the usual amount of exercise and food. Four to five weeks after mating, at which stage the unborn puppies start to take shape, they will begin to absorb sustenance from the dam. At this time the food intake should be increased, in particular using more protein or meat than previously given. This increase should be gradual, and by the time the bitch is due to whelp, approximately 2 lb of meat—plus, of course, the usual amount of biscuit meal, yeast and vitamins—should be given each day. It is best to divide this quantity into two separate meals so that the dam does not suffer from a distended stomach and can more easily absorb the food. The extra half-pound or so of meat is, of course, intended for the benefit of the embryo puppies and must not have the effect of putting weight on the bitch. The addition of an egg each day and a drink of milk can also be of benefit to the future litter.

During the second half of the gestation period, the bitch should be discouraged from jumping or taking too much exercise, although the usual daily walk can be maintained until the last week.

Let us assume that, as in the majority of cases, all is going well and the bitch's temperature has dropped from the normal 101·5°F to 99°F. This implies that within twenty-four hours she should start to give birth to her litter. Although it is not always easy to estimate exactly when the first puppy will be born, her general demeanour, expression and restlessness will give some indication.

First signs are that as the puppy enters the pelvis the dam will begin to strain, pant and, probably, tremble a little. Sometimes a puppy will follow within the next few minutes but quite often an hour or so will elapse before the birth occurs.

As each puppy is born it is natural for the bitch to break open the membrane or bag in which the puppy is encased and release it from her body by biting through the umbilical cord. Occasionally, especially if it is her first litter, she may neglect to take these steps. It is a simple matter to break the bag with finger and thumb so that the protective liquid can escape and the puppy is able to breathe, after which, using the sterilised scissors, the umbilical cord should be cut approximately 2 inches from the puppy's body. This should cause the youngster to squeak, then it must be quickly dried with a warm towel and placed on to a nipple.

Should the puppy be inert and obviously not breathing, it almost certainly means that mucus or some other obstruction is in the throat or nose. In such cases the body should be taken in one hand, held firmly by the hind quarters and with the head hanging downwards, shaken quite vigorously three or four times. This will remove the mucus and enable the puppy to breathe. Another method of resuscitation is to immerse the inert puppy three or four times alternately in warm and cold water, the shock effect of which often causes it to start breathing.

Should the puppy refuse to suckle, the following method will be of help. Press one of the dam's nipples until milk appears. With the other hand, using forefinger and thumb, gently squeeze the sides of the puppy's muzzle until the mouth opens, and then present it to the teat. Hold the puppy in this position until it realises that drink is at hand, when it should begin to suckle.

Incidentally, do not forget to have the sterilised scissors, towel and some soap close to hand prior to the birth of the first puppy, and I suggest that a packet of cigarettes and a flask of brandy or coffee should also be available because these could help you keep calm while the bitch is producing her litter.

Following the birth of each puppy, the bitch should extrude the placenta, or what is more commonly known as the after-birth. It is quite normal for the dam to eat or swallow this unsightly mess and some breeders consider that it helps clear up any impurities remaining in the bitch when whelping is completed.

Occasionally, especially after a prolonged period of straining, the bitch will stand up just at the moment of giving birth. Should this occur, you should quickly move the other puppies to one side of the whelping box before they are trampled or trodden on. Also be prepared to take hold of the puppy just as it is born because it may already be out of the membrane and the umbilical cord already severed. In these comparatively rare cases, the new-born puppy could hit the floor of the box if not caught in good time.

During the period of whelping the mother will probably refuse all food but will need copious drinks of milk or cool water containing glucose. This lack of appetite but continual desire for drink could last for a couple of days, so do make sure that plenty of liquid is available, especially as it encourages the production of milk in the dam. When the bitch recovers her appetite she should be given 2 lb of meat each day plus, of course, the usual quantity of biscuit meal and vitamins and yeast tablets. This should continue until the litter is weaned, when a return to the normal food intake can take place.

It is not always a certainty that a bitch will conceive and produce a litter sixty-three days after mating. At times she may have a false or phantom pregnancy, going through all the usual motions, even to the extent of swelling at the belly and producing milk. A bitch in this condition will then deflate on the sixty-third day leaving an empty nest and a very disappointed owner.

Although I have said that the full gestation period is nine weeks, there are occasions when the litter arrives two or three days earlier than expected. There are other times, however, when the dam, obviously in whelp, goes two or three days beyond the date on which the litter should be born. This could be caused by a dead puppy blocking the passage, or one incorrectly placed, which makes birth impossible or extremely difficult. Usually, puppies are born at fairly regular intervals of half an hour or so but at other times, periods of an hour or even two hours occur between births. Should the interval be protracted and the bitch after continuous straining produce no puppy, veterinary advice must urgently be sought. In all probability the vet will give an injection of Pituitrin which relaxes the bitch and usually the puppy is quickly born. More often than not I have seen twins born a few minutes after such an injection. There is the odd time, however, when the vet will advise a caesarean operation in order to extract as many live puppies as possible and save the mother's life.

Finally, and believe me this is good advice, do not allow visitors to see the litter or the dam for at least seven days after the puppies are born. I know full well that the average breeder is proud to show friends a new-born litter, and I also know of cases where the dam has resented such intrusion, become upset and nervy, and her milk has dried up.

PUPPY-REARING

Assuming that all has gone well for the dam, and your nerves, and that the bitch, whom nature has provided with warmth, love and food for her offspring, is happily rearing her litter, it is best to leave her well alone, apart from encouraging her to take a little exercise, when she will relieve herself and almost immediately rush back to her charges. Food, and plenty of it in liquid form, is an essential for the next couple of weeks. Barring unforeseen circumstances, the dam will be the sole provider of milk until the puppies reach the age of approximately three weeks. Nature and instinct provide the mother with food and warmth to dispense to her puppies and the less you interfere with this arrangement the better. Obviously, should the dam be ill or for any other reason unable to tend the litter, other steps must be taken, and it is always best to seek advice from your local vet if the dam is reticent about feeding her charges or the puppies are disinclined to feed voraciously.

With a normal size litter it is best to start feeding meat to the puppies at three weeks of age but if the litter is larger than usual, it is advisable to begin a little earlier. The first feed given to the puppies should consist of one teaspoonful of scraped raw meat and this quantity should be increased each day. On the third day two meat feeds should be given, not forgetting to increase the quantity each day until the puppies are four weeks old. At this stage milk, egg and glucose are introduced between the two meat feeds.

One week later the milk feeds should be thickened with Farex, or a similar cereal, the puppies now receiving two meat meals and two milk feeds, the latter containing Farex, eggs and glucose.

By now, the dam should be feeding the litter only at midday, last thing at night, and first thing in the morning, and by the time the puppies are six weeks old she should have finished with them entirely.

Remembering that the very small meat feed given at three weeks of age has to be rapidly increased, the puppies, by the time they reach six weeks, should be having 8 oz of meat and 1 pint of milk each day. When twelve weeks old, each puppy should be eating between $\frac{3}{4}$ and 1 lb of meat a day, which is still slowly increased until by the time the pups are six months $1\frac{1}{2}$ lb each should be the intake. From then on the meat meal can be decreased according to appetite and condition, as can also the number of meals each day.

All puppies can be fed together but this does not mean that they are left so that some take more than others. All must be carefully watched to make sure that each get its full share of the food. Give as much food as the puppies will readily eat and increase the amount every three days. When eight weeks old, the puppies' food should have a little Stress and halibut oil added to the meat, followed one week later with some bone flour.

It is about this time you should consider registering the puppies with the Kennel Club. A prescribed form is obtainable either by letter or telephone and is self-explanatory. Should it be your intention to breed several litters, it is a good idea to register your first with the initial A, second with B and so on, because this will enable you to keep track of the dogs bred in your own kennels as they grow older and enter the show ring. An approved affix or prefix can be given by the Kennel Club and I advise that this be obtained because, as time goes on, you will have the added thrill of seeing your breeding ideas perpetuated in print as and when each of the puppies bred in your kennels gains successes in the show ring or in obedience competition. Incidentally, prior to selling any of your litter, you will, of course, make sure that all puppies are free from worms and immunised against distemper, hardpad and possibly hepatitis. Worming these days is a painless operation and your vet will advise on the best medicament to use. This is usually based on the weight of the puppy, and modern science has given us several preparations that do not require starving the puppy prior to its use. It is advisable, even if no signs of worms are visible, to worm the litter when six weeks of age with a repetitive dose a week or so later.

Nobody seems to know why all puppies become infected with this parasite, because even if, as is usual, the dam and sire are free from this trouble, the puppies will nearly always develop worms. Immunisation against distemper and hardpad and hepatitis is essential because although the old dreaded days of distemper are almost gone, occasionally there are outbreaks in different parts of the country that can be devastating.

A tip worth remembering is to cut the ends of the puppies' nails once every week from the time they are one week old because if left long and sharp they will make the bitch very sore and often impatient.

Always make sure that as soon as the puppies are up on their feet and walking around, they have access to fresh air and sunshine, the ideal kennel having an open door leading to a good-sized run.

I would remind readers that the Standard requires the removal of dew claws and part of the tail, both operations taking place when the puppies are three to four days old. Dew claws are removed for two reasons. Firstly, when the Dobermann is adult these projections can become ingrown and if damaged, cause infection when the dog is running freely in a field, and liable to damage when turning quickly. Secondly, from the aesthetic viewpoint, a leg with no protruberance is much cleaner to look at than one with ugly dew claws sticking out from each of the front legs.

Tail docking is practised partly because a long tail can cause trouble to your furniture and table decorations if the exuberant Dobermann wags that appendage when greeting you each morn-

Ch. Tavey's Stormy Abundance

Barrimilne New Line Flor

Am. Ch. Kay Hill's Paint the Town Red

Ch. Kay Hill's Takeswon to Nowon

Ch. Rancho Dobe's Storm

Ch. Tavey's Stormy Wrath

Aust. Ch. Denecourt Ranch Mink, C.D.

Jan A. Johannesen

Int. Ch. Tavey's Stormy Nurmi (Norway)

ing and evening. More important still, it helps with the pleasing outline of a noble pedigree animal. Unless you know how to perform the operation of tail docking correctly, it is advisable to ask your vet to carry out the operation. In some cases it may be preferable for the breeder to offer advice to the vet before the removal takes place because it is often difficult to find at such a tender age exactly where the second joint of the tail is situated.

Most breeders retain approximately the width of a normal size pencil, only making the cut after a rubber band or narrow bandage has been tied as near to the root of the tail as is possible. This prevents bleeding and the band, or bandage, should be removed five minutes or so after cutting has taken place. A dab of permanganate of potash or an application of silver nitrate directly after the cutting has taken place should also help stop any bleeding from the dew claws and tail.

Do remember to use sterilised scissors when removing dew claws and tail because infection can be introduced if soiled tools are employed. It is also advisable for an assistant to take the mother away from the litter while the operation is being performed and not to return her to the whelping box until all bleeding has stopped. Some breeders I know use a tight rubber band when docking tails, this being placed at a position approximately ⅜ inch from the root. This rubber band is left on the tail for five to seven days and will slowly bite through the tail and eventually the excess portion will drop off.

Both methods have been used in my own kennels and I find that the rubber band system is easier to operate than cutting provided, of course, great care is taken in positioning the band and that it is drawn absolutely tight.

D

6

Common Ailments

You may think when reading this chapter, which covers a multitude of ailments and illnesses, that part of a dog's life must necessarily be spent with a veterinary surgeon. This is *not* so, because a dog that is healthy—and this greatly depends on the care and attention you lavish upon him, plus your own good sense of hygiene—should go through life with a minimum of medical attention.

Because of his resilience, the average dog is less prone to disease than humans, but as there is no medical health service for animals it behoves the owner to take every care of his companion so that large veterinary bills are not incurred. This does not mean that if and when your dog falls ill, and in order to save expense, you should revert to some of the 'home or granny's' remedies that have been tried out over the past many years. Your vet is an expert, having spent much time studying his profession and many more years in which experience has been gained, and he must be called in directly you fear that any serious illness has attacked your dog.

Tough as a Dobermann may be, he is just as liable to pick up disease as any other dog and it is only by carefully watching his condition, and with the aid of a veterinary surgeon, that your dog can be kept in top-class condition. It is always advisable to have a thermometer in your dog kit, especially if your Dobermann is young, at which time he is, of course, more prone to ailments than when older. Strange as it may seem, the normal temperature of a dog is 101·5°F and no matter what the weather conditions may be, a dog when fit and well will maintain this figure. The method of taking an animal's temperature is to use a blunt-ended thermometer and, after shaking the mercury content down to below 101°F, dip the end in Vaseline, or something similar, and then insert this into the rectum for a minute or two. Any definite rise above the normal, even as little as 1°F, allied to a general 'off colour' appearance, lassitude, loss of appetite, excessive drinking or vomiting indicates the need for veterinary advice.

I suppose the condition that most attacks dogs these days is worm infection but as this is intended as a reference chapter, it is best I think if the ailments to which dogs are liable are listed in alphabetical order.

ANAL GLANDS. Many dogs, especially those whose motions are loose over a space of time, need to have the secretion contained in the anal glands removed. Indications are similar to those of a puppy with worms, when he rubs his behind along the ground or when he continually licks the anus. It is a simple matter to remove the excess secretion from the glands, which are situated one on either side just inside the anus, by squeezing it out with finger and thumb. Take great care, however, to keep your body well away from the rear of the dog because at times the evil-smelling liquid can squirt out a couple of feet. Should the anal glands be persistently troublesome, it is advisable to have them surgically removed.

CANKER. This is, in effect, an inflammation inside the ear which, if neglected, not only causes the dog to suffer unduly but also emits a most objectionable smell. Symptoms are noticed when the dog continually scratches at the ear or shakes the head. One form of canker is known as otitis and can be caused by lack of attention on the part of the owner. Common causes of otitis are eczema, grass seeds and a particular type of mange, the mite of which only affects ears. Treatment in early cases consists of antibiotics, soothing preparations applied inside the ears and, if possible, the removal of any foreign body causing the irritation. Warm liquid paraffin is a useful home treatment to soothe the ears. A sedative is sometimes necessary to keep the dog calm and should prevent his damaging the appendage. In chronic cases it is best to seek veterinary advice because an operation to remove the cause may be essential. Finally, the dog's ears should be regularly cleaned by using a solution of Dettol or T.C.P. making sure that these appendages are well dried inside after the liquid has been used. A good method of drying the inaccessible parts of the ear is to cover the tip of an orange stick with cotton wool and to rotate it gently inside the ear, taking care not to probe too deeply.

CHOREA. This is nearly always an aftermath of distemper and is recognised by a twitching of the muscles in any part of the body.

CONJUNCTIVITIS. This is an easily detectable eye complaint because the cornea will show signs of inflammation caused either by a foreign body, distemper or entropion. The eyes will have the appearance of being half closed, the whites will redden and the membranes will swell. In order to relieve itself of pain the dog may scratch the affected eye, or eyes, with his paw and even try to rub himself along the ground. Sometimes a bluish film will partly cover the eye, which condition indicates hepatitis or a corneal ulcer. Temporary relief can be given by using Golden Eye Ointment but veterinary advice is most desirable.

COUGH. Coughing can denote any of a multitude of troubles and is evident in distemper, bronchitis, pneumonia and even the absorption of sawdust, which is so often used in puppy kennels. Relief can be given by means of aspirin or codeine every three to four hours, but veterinary advice must be sought in order to find out the cause before a definite cure can be made.

CRYPTORCHIDISM. This is a condition in which both testicles are not descended into the scrotum. It is a hereditary fault and an animal so handicapped cannot reproduce. The Kennel Club will not issue an Export Certificate for such males unless the purchaser definitely states that he is aware of the fault. Usually, and in most breeds, the testicles should have descended into the scrotum by the time the dog is six months old, but should this not be the case, veterinary science these days can often assist.

CUTS. If the slit or wound is small, the application of diluted Dettol, T.C.P. or similar antiseptic should suffice, but if there is a definite rip or tear, the hair should be cut away from the damaged area and after washing away any impurities, penicillin should be injected into the aperture. Should the wound be of a size to need stitches, the dog must be hurried to the vet before septicaemia sets in. Venous bleeding, i.e. that which comes from a vein, is dark red in colour and can be arrested by applying a reasonably tight bandage over the wound until the bleeding stops. More serious, however, is arterial bleeding which will be seen as spurts of bright red blood denoting that an artery has been torn or damaged. While waiting for the vet to take over, the haemorrhage should be controlled by applying a tourniquet above the wound nearer to the heart, releasing after five minutes or so for several seconds to allow the circulation to continue and then retying the tourniquet.

CYSTITIS. A growth, stone or simple inflammation can cause this bladder trouble and a minor operation by a vet can give a lasting cure. Symptoms are that the dog will try to pass urine more often than normally, at times being unable to make any water at all, and at others showing blood streaks in the urine.

DIARRHOEA. Many people make light of this condition, considering it to be a passing sickness. Such is not always the case and it should be treated quite seriously. Possible causes are infection of some form or other, the result of having eaten something unsuitable such as decomposed food or filth, or perhaps the symptoms may denote the onset of distemper. Occasionally, the motion, which is of course very loose, may be tinged with blood or contain blobs of mucus. Should this be apparent, a vet should immediately be summoned and while waiting for his arrival a tablespoon of Kaolin powder or a strinacin tablet could be given three to four times a day. Directly after treatment all red meat should be excluded from the daily meal for four or five days so that the stomach is fully rested. The food should be reasonably dry, that is to say without too much gravy or similar liquid, and should be given little and often. Provided it does not cause the dog to vomit, he may be given as much to drink as he wishes, this preventing dehydration. It is important that a sample of the stools and a full report on the condition should be available for the vet when he calls.

DISTEMPER. This is a virus disease and, fortunately, in these days is not the dreaded scourge it was fifteen years ago. It is essential that all puppies be inoculated against this when about three months of age, especially as the sickness is contagious. Allied to distemper are the diseases known as hardpad and contagious hepatitis, but here again, because of the progress in veterinary science, it has been combatted by inoculation and is not as greatly feared as it was ten years ago. Symptoms of distemper and hardpad are very similar, the main distinction being that if the latter is allowed to run its course there is a definite hardening of the pads and nose in the afflicted animal. Both diseases start with a dry cough, running eyes and nose, and possible retching, with the temperature rising to 104° or 105°F. General depression and loss of appetite are also noticed and unless veterinary assistance is quickly obtained the dog will die or at best be affected in the nose and brain, causing chorea or paralysis. Immediate isolation of any dog suspected of distemper or hardpad is absolutely essential, otherwise the disease will spread right through the kennels. I cannot too strongly emphasise that it is your duty to your dog and also to those of your neighbours to have your puppy immunised at the age of three months, at which age antibodies will not interfere with the vaccine, and in addition most serious breeders give a booster injection every other year, otherwise the dog's immunity may wane. It is usual to immunise against both distemper and hardpad in one injection. Contagious hepatitis virus primarily attacks the liver and can cause sudden death. Sometimes, however, it results in a rise in temperature with only a slight malaise. Symptoms are that the eye surface becomes blue and opaque, which clears in a few days.

A bitch can become a carrier of hepatitis and it is this disease that is often the cause of fading puppies. Inoculation against hepatitis can be given at the same time as that for distemper and hardpad.

ECLAMPSIA. Often called milk fever, this condition can cause rapid decline and death. It usually occurs during the first three days after the litter is born and is, in effect, a severe lack of calcium in the bloodstream of the bitch, due to her failure to draw on calcium reserves in her body. It can, however, occur any time during lactation and, even if treated early on, can recur as the puppies grow older and take more out of the dam. Symptoms are that the bitch will become nervous, irritable, restless and apprehensive and the puppies will show similar traits. If left too long without expert attention, the bitch will develop fits and convulsions, from which moment the cure will be very difficult. If taken in time, the vet will give injections of calcium to balance the deficiency which can effect a complete and almost miraculous cure. A bitch who has had eclampsia should be most carefully watched at future whelping because this condition is very likely to occur again. To help prevent a recurrence of eclampsia, it is advisable to wean the puppies as early as possible to reduce the drain of calcium in the bitch.

ECZEMA. Great care must be taken not to confuse this with mange, of which there are several different forms. Eczema can be dry or wet, according to the cause, and is detectable by lack of hair around the affected parts. Eczema is due to skin irritation caused by an allergic reaction of the dog to some external cause. It can also be caused by faulty feeding or kennel management and can even be hereditary. An excess of carbohydrates such as biscuit, bread, etc., is a common cause of eczema and it is worth while trying a reduction of such foods should the disease be suspected. The affected parts are usually on the belly, shanks and legs and are more often than not aggravated by the dog continually licking the affected areas. A dressing of calamine lotion several times a day with the addition of an 'Elizabethan collar' fixed securely around the neck of the patient could clear the condition. Should it persist, you must expect something more serious than eczema, and obtain veterinary advice.

ENTROPION. This is a hereditary defect and I must impress upon owners that breeding from dogs with this complaint should not be practised. Symptoms are that the lower eyelid rolls inwards causing the lashes to irritate the eyes, and the condition becomes progressively worse unless a minor operation is performed.

EYE MUCUS. For some reason, unknown to me, many short-haired dogs such as Boxers, Dobermanns and Dachshunds seem to suffer more from this trouble than do the longer-haired varieties. Usually, there is really nothing serious in this condition and a regular washing out with a saline solution, followed by the application of a recommended eye ointment into the corner of each eye can effect a remedy. It must, however, be remembered that the piece of cotton-wool used to introduce the saline solution into each eye should be discarded and not used on the second eye after the first has been treated. It is best if the cotton-wool is soaked in the saline solution and then allowed to drip into the corner of the eyes, when the mucus will easily float out and the offending matter can be wiped away.

FITS. Fits or violent muscular spasms are caused by a variety of reasons, and while some are almost harmless, others can be very dangerous. An infestation of worms can bring on an attack and so can teething fits, which usually occur at about the age of three to four months when the second set of teeth are replacing the first or baby teeth. The convulsions can be really alarming, occasionally causing complete loss of consciousness, which is in effect a coma. Usually, if the fits are caused by an infestation of worms, the removal of the parasites will clear up the condition. An attack of distemper will also cause fits and if the sickness reaches such a stage, there is a distinct risk of chorea setting in afterwards. Further symptoms are frothing at the mouth and much looseness of bladder and bowels and a threshing of the limbs, while the jaws are held rigidly tight. Do nothing to bring the puppy out of its fit except to wrap it in a towel in a warm room while an urgent call is made to a veterinary surgeon. Tranquillisers often cut down the frequency of attacks but I must repeat that your vet must be summoned so that the cause can be eliminated, after which the dog will lead a happy normal life.

FLEAS. There is little that can be written about fleas in Dobermanns because being short-coated and lacking in undercoat, the conditions under which fleas live do not easily occur in our breed. However, there may be the odd occasion when fleas can be found on a Dobermann coat and, if neglected, a severe irritation will be set up, causing dry sores that have the appearance of eczema. A sprinkling of Gammexine insecticide powder applied every three or four days should soon clear the trouble and an application of the same powder to the dog bedding should prevent a recurrence. Here again it is a matter of strict hygiene that will help your dog live a happy, contented and carefree life.

FRACTURES. There is little one can do in the case of fractures or dislocations except to seek immediate veterinary assistance. Do not attempt to apply a splint, and if taking the dog to a vet yourself, make sure that he is wrapped in a warm blanket, keeping him as still as possible and supporting the injured section by hand. Dogs, being the brave creatures they are, often still attempt to move around even when a severe dislocation or fracture has taken place. Sometimes a swelling around the damaged part will be noticed, the dog may attempt to move on three legs and there will be audible evidence of pain. This is the time to check for any break, sprain or dislocation and, if in any doubt at all, contact the vet at once.

GASTRITIS. Although gastritis is simply an irritation of the stomach, the condition must be treated as something quite serious. It can be caused by infection, by an ingestion of filth, or a foreign body. Urgent attention is required before a much worse condition sets in. The symptoms are continual vomiting even after all food has been disposed of, while a frothy fluid, tinged with blood, will at times be ejected. A saline emetic may be necessary and it is possible that the vet will decide to use a stomach pump. This is a skilled job of work, necessitating the introduction of a long rubber tube via the throat into the stomach and must be undertaken by a professional and certainly not by an amateur. Further symptoms are an intense thirst, but it will be impossible for the dog to retain the liquid and will vomit it back again almost immediately. It is obvious that a dog continually losing all food and liquid quickly becomes dehydrated, which condition, unless immediately remedied, can cause death. Should there for any reason be a long wait before the dog can be seen by a vet, a mixture of kaolin or chlorodyne to the amount of one tablespoonful can be given every four hours. Further than this, all food and liquid must be withheld and the patient should be kept in a warm temperature.

HARDPAD. *See* Distemper.

HEPATITIS. This is another virus infection, immunisation against which should be given at the same time as the distemper and hard-pad injections. Puppies contracting this disease have little chance of survival and die very quickly. Symptoms are vomiting, convulsions and violent diarrhoea and the patient must be kept very warm until the vet has had a chance to see it. (*See also* Distemper.)

HIP DYSPLASIA. This is a hereditary condition of the hip joint, the ball and socket of which are malformed. The only certain way to find whether or not the dog is suffering from hip dysplasia is by X-ray, although symptoms are such as to make recognition reasonably easy. The fault lies in the fact that the ball at the top of the lower thigh bone does not fit correctly into the socket of the upper thigh bone which is too flat as distinct from being hollow to enable free and easy movement to take place. This is visible when the dog is moving across your vision, there being a lame, stilted and awkward action instead of complete freedom of movement. In advanced cases, a distinct click can be heard when the dog is running nearby and if after X-ray the condition is diagnosed definitely as hip dysplasia, no serious and conscientious breeder would consider using the affected dog or its sire or dam for further breeding.

HOOK-WORMS. These, as distinct from the round-worm and tapeworm that feeds on predigested food, are of the blood-sucking species whose heads are fitted with teeth with which they hang on to the host's intestines where they happily suck away at the blood cells. Symptoms are the same as those for round-worms, but the damage they can cause is infinitely greater. Hook-worms are very small creatures and can only be discovered by having the motions tested. Treatment by a qualified vet is essential before complete elimination can be effected. Luckily, hook-worms are not common in Britain, although they are in tropical and subtropical climates.

LEPTOSPIROSIS. This disease, which is similar to yellow jaundice, is usually contracted from rat urine and it is for that reason it has been found advisable to change the dog's drinking water and remove all bones and left-over food every morning before the dogs are allowed out of the kennels. A dog with this sickness will show loss of appetite and an incredible thirst. The gums and whites of the eyes will develop a yellowish tinge, liver and kidneys will be attacked, the dog will develop a high temperature, and blood will be vomited and passed through the back passage. Unless immediate veterinary attention is obtained, the dog will die, so here again it is essential that immunisation be given at the same time as the distemper and hardpad inoculation. In cases that recover from this dread disease a long period of convalescence is necessary and the damage to the kidneys could be such as to cause chorea when the dog reaches middle age.

LICE. It must be remembered that while fleas breed in a dog's bedding, lice actually breed on the dog itself and burrow under the skin. An insecticide bath will kill lice and it is essential that it be repeated about ten days later to kill the remainder that will hatch out from eggs laid under the skin. To make absolutely sure that all the parasites have been eliminated a further bath seven days later is advisable and the bedding should be changed.

MANGE. There are two primary types of mange, one being sarcoptic and the other demodectic or follicular. The former, which is contagious, is usually detected inside the thighs, under the armpits, on the belly and around the head, neck and ears. Slightly raised red pimples will cause a coloration of the skin, there will be a loss of coat, and the dog will continually scratch the infected areas. Gammexine applied every three or four days over a period of four weeks will help relieve the condition, and while this disease was dreaded some few years ago, modern veterinary science can these days affect a cure. It is, however, a long process, and veterinary advice must be strictly adhered to. It must be remembered that there is always a possibility of re-infection from the dog's surroundings, so the bedding should be changed and any blankets boiled at least once a week while treatment is being given. Demodectic mange, also caused by a mite that eats its way under the skin of the affected animal, carries the same symptoms as sarcoptic, but is less contagious. However, the condition is serious because of irritation to the dog, unsightly bald patches followed by rawness and thickening of the skin. Treatment is the same as that for sarcoptic mange although the cure can take rather longer to effect. Demodectic mange is usually caught from the nursing mother, although noticeable rawness may not be spotted until long after the whelps have left the dam.

METRITIS. Retained afterbirth, dead foetuses and bacterial infection can cause an inflammation of the uterus, setting up metritis which usually appears three or four days after whelping a litter. The temperature will rise; there will be a bad smelling discharge from the vulva, milk production will dry up and in any case be affected, all of which means that expert veterinary advice is immediately required.

MONORCHIDISM. This is exactly the same as cryptorchidism except that one testicle is descended into the scrotum, and it is possible to breed from a sire with this condition. However, it is considered that this fault is inherited and the Kennel Club will not issue an export pedigree for such males unless the purchaser states that he is aware of the fault. Obviously it is wrong to breed from monorchid dogs or from bitches that repeatedly produce such puppies and no breeding programme should permit the use of such sires or dams.

NEPHRITIS. A dog with nephritis, which is an inflammation of the kidneys, will show signs of extreme thirst which should be regulated by giving barley water instead of ordinary water, the

mixture being two heaped tablespoonsful of pearl barley allowed
to soak in boiling water, well stirred, strained and then allowed
to cool. The food intake must also be regulated and very little
protein given while the symptoms are present. Small doses of
food at frequent intervals are advisable, so that the kidneys are
not overloaded at any one time.

PHANTOM PREGNANCY. For some reason, unknown to me,
Dobermanns seem to develop this condition far more often than
do most other breeds. This occurs after a bitch has been in season
with no mating affected, and whether it is because the Dobermann is oversexed or nature is taking its course, she will often go
through all the symptoms of being in whelp. At about six weeks
after her season, her abdomen will swell, just as if she were carrying a litter and in another couple of weeks, the mammary glands
will enlarge, the nipples will grow bigger and milk can be
extracted. A week or so later she will make a bed and give every
sign of preparing for a litter. On due date she will deflate and the
milk supply dry up, and this is the time to call in your vet so that
a thorough check can be made just to make sure that there are no
deleterious after-effects. A phantom pregnancy can also occur
after a definite mating has taken place and no obvious conception
has been achieved. If this is the case, it is advisable, and even
essential, that your vet be consulted because bitches can absorb
the foetus early on in pregnancy, which condition must have
expert treatment.

POISON. It is quite an easy matter, especially if the owner does
not exercise sufficient care, for a dog to pick up and ingest any of
several poisonous substances. If there is the slightest reason for
suspecting that a poison has been absorbed, there are several ways
in which immediate treatment or alleviation from pain can be
given while waiting for veterinary advice. Acids such as nitric,
hydrochloric, and sulphuric can be temporarily neutralised by
forcing diluted bicarbonate of soda down the throat. In addition
aludrux can be used while waiting for veterinary assistance. Do
not attempt to use an emetic such as washing soda, because this
can worsen the condition. Strychnine and arsenic: these two

poisons can kill the dog within half an hour unless an emetic such as a strong saline solution or epsom salts are given immediately after the poison has been taken. In most cases there is little chance of survival. Make sure that vomiting occurs at the earliest possible moment so that at least part of the poison is ejected, keep the dog warm and as restful as possible while waiting for the vet, who if told of the suspected trouble, will call with the least possible delay.

PROGRESSIVE RETINAL ATROPHY. This disease usually affects older dogs and is often referred to as night blindness or P.R.A. Most veterinary surgeons claim that P.R.A. is inherent and the very word progressive means exactly what it says. It is claimed that the progeny of dogs afflicted with this blindness are born with the disease, which can take up to two years before correct diagnosis can be made. I doubt whether there is any cure for P.R.A. and the way to eliminate it is not to breed from dogs or bitches suspected of carrying this trait. It is, as I have said before, a progressive disease and invariably a dog who has inherited it will go completely blind by the time it is seven or eight years old.

Much research into this illness has been made by Dr K. C. Barnett, M.R.C.V.S., and his findings have been of great benefit and education to veterinary science. It is possible to discover whether or not a dog is suffering from P.R.A. with an ophthalmoscope, but as it needs a specialist vet to interpret his findings, it is best if such an expert were consulted.

PYOMETRA. This is a form of metritis that occurs approximately two months after the bitch starts a season. It occurs more often in bitches that have never had a litter and usually happens from the age of seven years onwards. Symptoms are that the bitch will go off her food, she will drink a lot, and may possibly discharge a pink pus. If there is no discharge, the other symptoms could be more acute and the bitch may die within a few days. If the discharge is copious, the other symptoms will be less acute. The only effective treatment is surgical removal of ovaries and uterus.

RAT POISON. Not all of these preparations are harmless to dogs, some containing phosphorus, strychnine, arsenic or like poisons. Rats are extremely tough animals and if the poison used to kill them is also absorbed by a dog, especially a puppy, a similar result can be expected. It is essential that veterinary advice and treatment be obtained at the earliest possible moment if such poisoning is suspected.

ROUND-WORMS. Usually these attack younger dogs although older animals can also be infected. Worms cause little trouble in adults but can cause serious troubles in puppies which should be treated at the age of six weeks. They are white or milky in colour, round in cross-section, can be of varying lengths and often, when extruded, can be a mass as big as a handful. They can live in the stomach, intestines, heart and rectum but if the correct worming medicament is given according to weight and on the advice of your vet, little trouble should be experienced. It is advisable that worming medicine be given twice to each suspected dog at intervals of ten days. Fortunately, modern treatments are mild, safe and effective. It is advisable to worm the bitch at the beginning and half way through pregnancy as puppies are infected from the bitch and such worming reduces the burden on the puppies. Symptoms of worms are usually a harsh coat, depraved appetite, yawning, vomiting, diarrhoea, fits due to indigestion or distention of the stomach, often allied to the animal developing a habit of sitting down and pulling himself along with the front legs, thus scraping his bottom along the ground.

STINGS. These are more common than dog owners suspect, mainly because the Dobermann, being of an inquisitive nature, will often put his head into a wasps' nest or attempt to bite the bee that is worrying him. Usually such stings are not highly dangerous and the effects wear off within twenty-four hours. However, if the sting is in the mouth, throat or on the tongue, the resultant swelling could be dangerous and veterinary attention should be sought. If the bee sting is left in the skin and is visible, it should be removed with a pair of fine tweezers, and an alkali such as a teaspoon of washing soda dissolved in a quarter-pint of water should be dabbed on the affected part. Wasp stings can

be treated with a cut lemon but if the origin of the sting is unknown, treatment as suggested for the bee sting should be
adopted.

TAPEWORMS. These horrible parasites are usually harder to
eliminate than round-worms and if the dog is left untreated it can
die or suffer irreparable harm. They are white in colour, flat in
cross-section and can measure anything up to ten yards long.
Their main habitat is in the intestines, and when the condition
becomes acute, segments can be seen and found in the dog's
motions or protruding from the hindquarters. The full worm is
normally only seen when a vermifuge has caused it to be passed.
It must be quite a life to be a tapeworm until the veterinary surgeon starts to use his emetic because all they do is to lie in the gut
or intestines surrounded by warm liquid and pre-digested food,
thinking only of procreation. However, these are dangerous parasites and the sooner the dog is rid of them the better. Symptoms
of tapeworms are rather similar to those for round-worms, the
main differences being that the breath smells badly and the appetite tends towards devouring filth. Emaciation will show an advanced stage of infestation, as will also the 'tucked up' belly
appearance. Paralysis of the hindquarters can also be caused if the
condition is neglected.

TICKS. Fortunately, we in Britain do not suffer to anything like
the same extent as do breeders in Australia, the United States of
America and other parts of the world from ticks. It is rare that
ticks are found in England and when such an attack does occur, it
is invariably in country disticts. Ticks are easily seen on short-
coated dogs such as Dobermanns because small lumps are raised
on and under the skin, these being caused by the parasite feeding
on the animal's blood and becoming bloated. The method of removing these vampires is to apply cotton-wool soaked in ether
or surgical spirit and holding it over the affected part for a few
minutes. The tick will then die and can be removed with a pair of
fine tweezers, great care being taken to remove all of the body,
particularly the head which, if left, will cause soreness and possible
infection.

TONSILLITIS. This is more often a symptom of other ailments than a disease in itself. It can be caused by either bacterial or virus infection and is detected by inflammation of the tonsils which will be reddened and enlarged. Coughing, vomiting and lack of appetite lead one to suspect tonsillitis which, being a symptom of something more serious, should receive urgent veterinary attention.

WORMS. *See* Hook-worms, Round-worms, Tapeworms.

7
Showing

THIS part of dogdom can become most rewarding because both you and your dog can derive much pleasure from competition even if you do not continually win prizes. A host of new friends will come your way and once your dog has learnt what is expected from him he will enter into the spirit of the thing and look forward to meeting other representatives of his breed.

A champion bitch I once owned needed no posing in the show ring. Having learnt exactly what was expected of her she took great delight in holding her stance while photographers took flash pictures, relaxing when she knew their work was finished.

There are several types of dog shows in Britain, all governed by the Kennel Club, ranging from sanction to championship shows and it is only at the latter that challenge certificates are awarded. Much enjoyment can be obtained at the smaller shows, but championship shows are, of course, more important. So that I can more easily explain the system of judging adopted at all shows, let us assume that you have a first-class specimen already registered at the Kennel Club, and follow him through the recognised procedure.

First of all, check whether or not you transferred the dog from the name of the breeder to your own. This is essential, because no dog is eligible to compete at a show run under Kennel Club rules unless registered in the name of the owner. Buy one or both of the weekly dog magazines, *Dog World* and *Our Dogs*, in which forthcoming shows will be advertised. Make sure that the Dobermann breed is scheduled and then write to the show secretary, whose name and address will appear in the advertisement, and ask for a schedule and entry form. The schedule will set out and explain the qualifications for each class and also state the entry fee.

The entry form, together with your cheque, must be sent to the show secretary before closing date, which is usually approximately one month before the show takes place. The classification varies from show to show but in the case of Dobermanns usually covers ten or more classes at championship shows, separated according to age groups, past successes and sex. Let us assume that the dog you are exhibiting is fifteen months of age and has never been shown before which means, of course, that he is eligible for the junior class which is for exhibits of less than eighteen months of age. He is not eligible for the puppy class, which is confined to dogs aged between six and twelve months. He can also compete in the novice class, not having previously won a first prize and, of course, being proud of him as you are, he must be entered in the open dog class which, as the name implies, is open to all male exhibits of his breed.

A certain amount of preparation and ring training is undoubtedly essential, but I shall deal with that later in this chapter. All championship shows are benched which, in effect, means that every exhibit has its own particular bench on which to rest and the only times he can be removed is while being exercised (for a maximum period of fifteen minutes) or while being shown in the ring. There is also a Kennel Club regulation relating to the time of arrival and to the time of departure from the show, both of which must be rigidly observed.

Now you are ready for the competition, and this being your first attempt, a few butterflies move around in your stomach. Get rid of these as soon as you can because, believe me, the temperament of the handler is so easily transmitted to the dog. Happily, your Dobermann feels perfectly at ease because he likes being with you and seeing the other fellows. He stands up proudly, moves very well and to your pleasure and excitement, the judge awards you the first prize. Out of the ring you go, feeling cock-a-hoop with it all and start grooming the dog for the next class. Into the ring you both go once again and out you come with another first prize. Anxiously you wait for the open dog class, not without a little fear and trepidation, all of which was quite unfounded because once again the first prize is yours. Now we come to the elimination part of the competition and if there is another male exhibit which has remained unbeaten in other classes, he may compete against you for best dog. Amidst claps and cheers from your new-found friends, you win the contest and are awarded your first challenge certificate. There is more elimination to come because the Dobermann that was awarded the bitch challenge certificate will compete with you for best of breed. Keep calm and take advice from the other exhibitors who have noticed just how much the judge has fallen for your dog. Into the ring you go with new-found confidence and finish up with the coveted rosette, which proclaims to all and sundry that in the opinion of this particular judge you have the best Dobermann exhibit of the day.

Now for a word of warning. Judges quite rightly interpret standards in slightly different ways and, therefore, have different opinions of what constitutes the perfect Dobermann. Inevitably, in the not too distant future you will come across one who will prefer another exhibit to yours. Do not get a swelled head because of your dog's early successes; he can change, you can be off-colour, and as I have already said, judges' opinions differ. However, continuing with the assumption that this is your day, and having won the best of breed award in Dobermanns you are entitled to compete for best in show.

First you must win the group reserved for working dog exhibits and, having won this, there is time to rest while the winners of the other five groups are selected. We now reach the most important part of the contest. Your Dobermann and the winners of Hound, Toy, Terrier, Gundog and Utility groups go into the final competition from which a judge selects his ultimate best in show.

Now let us go back to the beginning of the chapter and consider preparation and ring training. No hard and fast rule can be applied to such work, because each and every dog is an individual needing specialised treatment according to its character, temperament and conformation. However, a few hints on preparation for the show ring may be of interest to exhibitors.

The first thing to bear in mind is that training begins from the day your prospective champion leaves its dam. Your puppy must quickly become acclimatised to noises and contact with strange people, which it will experience at dog shows.

Handle your puppy at every opportunity. Stroke it while feeding, playing and even while sleeping in the nest, because in this way the youngster will become used to interference at all times.

Throw metal tins down while the puppy is playing around in the garden, because this will improve its temperament and accustom it to extraneous noises, which are the bugbear at all shows.

Soon you will have your Dobermann full of pluck and prepared to ignore the judge when under manual examination.

Next you must teach your exhibit to stand still while being shown, and this is best done by placing it on a low table standing something like 18 inches from the ground. Start by placing the front legs in the desired position and, without losing what I call manual contact with the body, slide your hands along the back and sides to the hindquarters, then quietly and firmly place the rear legs in the correct position, which incidentally should be the normal Dobermann stance, showing that the puppy can cover sufficient ground without over-angulation.

Of course, the youngster may first of all resent this treatment and attempt to jump from the table, but a little perseverance on the part of the handler will soon overcome its fears. A caress or pat on the shoulder soon teaches the dog to stand perfectly still after it has been properly positioned.

Most of my show dogs have become so used to being groomed and handled that they happily leap on to the low table used in our kennels, when allowed into the paddock, while their runs are being cleaned each morning and afternoon.

Now for gait. This is the part where the handler can get the most out of his dog. Study your exhibit and you will find that it moves better at certain speeds than others. Very few young Dobermanns will move correctly at both slow and fast speeds, so find out which best suits your puppy and concentrate on that particular action.

I find that if all whiskers and those odd hairs above the eyes, on the cheeks, and beneath the chin are removed, the judge, when looking at the dog's head, gains a better impression of strength of muzzle etc. Whiskers and hairs tend to spoil the effect of a well-filled foreface and nicely made skull which, after all, is what the judge is looking for. Longish and often straggly hairs also grow

down the back of the front legs, under the belly, at the rear of the
rump and down the back legs, so trim them away so that your dog
has a clean and neat appearance. This is easily effected with
clippers, scissors or a lighted taper, although great care must be
taken in using the latter method.

The preparation I have so far mentioned must, of course, be
undertaken the day before the show, leaving the final touch-up
until about half an hour prior to judging. This is the moment when
you get the shine on your dog, and I find that the following
treatment gives good results.

A good rub-down with witch hazel going the way of the hair
will remove all dust from the coat and, if only a little is used, it
will dry out in a minute or so. A very small quantity of Vaseline
hair tonic or similar preparation smeared over the palms of the
hands should be rubbed in, again going the way of the coat, with
particular attention to the feet and toenails. A final polish with a
chamois leather or piece of Turkish towelling should make your
Dobermann look bright and healthy.

From then onwards it is up to you; into the ring you will go,
together with your dog and, believe me, he will be just as nervous
or confident as you yourself feel. It is uncanny how the temperament of the handler is transmitted down the lead to the dog. So
do not fuss him unduly. Do not make him stand for a long time
in any one position. Give him a pat or two while waiting your
turn to go into the centre of the ring. Talk to him a little to keep
his interest alive and generally make him feel that, after all, this is
not so much different from having fun at home.

Most clubs offer special prizes either for best of breed, best dog,
best bitch or best puppy and I suggest that this is one of the
reasons, albeit a minor one, why you should join one of the five
Dobermann Clubs in Britain. (*See* Appendix B.)

In addition to the special prizes awarded at shows you will, by
being a member of the club, meet other enthusiasts at social
occasions as well as in the show ring—all of which makes life for
the Dobermaniac more enjoyable.

Early in this chapter I mentioned competition at Championship
level but there are, of course, several other types of shows at

which your dog will undoubtedly compete. These range from what are termed exemption shows right through to championship shows, so it may be helpful at least to the newcomer to have each defined.

EXEMPTION SHOWS. As the name implies, these are exempt from Kennel Club regulations and are usually organised in conjunction with a local fête or similar event. At these shows there are usually separate classes for sporting, terrier, toy and working groups, in the last of which a Dobermann may compete. In addition, there are usually classes for pet dogs and even cross-breeds, plus the more amusing competitions such as 'Dog with the longest tail', 'Dog in best condition', 'Dog that most suits the owner', and many others.

Exemption shows are really fun shows and while any award gained is not taken into account by the Kennel Club, many owners use such competitions to teach youngsters what is expected of them in the show ring.

SANCTION SHOWS. This type of show is restricted to members of a society and all exhibits must be registered at the Kennel Club. Such shows invariably consist of variety classes only, which means that all breeds are eligible for the classes which are governed by the group in which the breed is registered, age and any previous awards.

Neither challenge certificate winners, nor those who have won beyond what is termed the post-graduate class are eligible. Entry fees and prize money at sanction shows are invariably lower than those for the more important competitions.

LIMITED SHOWS. This is very similar to the sanction show, the main difference being that more often than not separate classes for several breeds are scheduled in addition to the usual variety classes. Entry fees and prize money are usually the same as those for sanction shows but less than those for open and championship shows.

OPEN SHOWS. As the title implies, these are open to all dogs from puppies to champions. Of course, these, as with all others apart from exemption shows, are held under Kennel Club rules. Open shows can range between one hundred and three hundred classes, the majority of which are confined to breeds, and the larger events are, because of a Kennel Club ruling, benched, which in effect means that each and every exhibit must be kept on its own specially allocated bench for the duration of the show unless it is actually competing in a class or being exercised for a maximum of fifteen minutes. Open shows are very popular with exhibitors because a first prize won in a breed class counts as one point towards a junior warrant. This is a special award given by the Kennel Club to dogs who have won twenty-five points prior to the age of eighteen months, there being, besides the one point gained at open shows, three such points for first prize awards at championship shows.

CHAMPIONSHIP SHOWS. These are the events at which Kennel Club challenge certificates are awarded, one for best dog in the breed and another for best bitch. Most championship shows schedule anything between sixty and one hundred different breeds, offering classes according to age and previous wins. At the moment there are twenty all-breed shows in Britain each year at which challenge certificates for Dobermanns can be won, plus five specialist shows organised by Dobermann clubs at which certificates are also awarded. Three such awards under three different judges entitles the dog to the title of champion.

These challenge certificates are awarded to the exhibits which in the opinion of the judge are 'worthy of the title of champion', but there are the very rare occasions when a judge withholds the certificate simply because he is not satisfied with the quality of his best dog or bitch and will not add his signature to the document.

OBEDIENCE CLASSES. Most championship shows provide classes for obedience in addition to those for beauty. These are graded according to previous wins and at the highest point, namely Test C, obedience championship certificates are awarded. As with the normal breed class competition, three first placings gained without losing more than ten from the maximum number of points, all gained under three different judges, qualifies the dog as an obedience champion. The only exception to this is at the annual Cruft's Show where the winner, who must have previously won at least one challenge certificate, automatically acquires the much valued title. There are literally hundreds of obedience societies in Britain holding regular weekly classes to teach dogs this highly specialised work, concentrating mainly on the set exercises as laid down by the Kennel Club.

8

The Dobermann in Obedience

THE Dobermann breed clubs in the United Kingdom have from the start given support to those members who enjoy training as well as showing their dogs. Indeed, the clubs or their branches have where possible organised training classes, provided a suitable trainer and a good nucleus of members could be found. Most of the Dobermanns trained by their owners have, however, attended those classes open to all breeds, which are run by societies formed in all parts of the country in response to increasing general interest in dog-training. With a capable and sympathetic instructor to give advice on problems as well as guidance in the basic principles of control a well-run class can be enjoyable and worth while. A Dobermann particularly enjoys sharing in any activity with its owner and successful training leads to a closer and more understanding relationship between them. Indeed, it is felt by those who have trained their own that the home life of many more Dobermanns would be happier had their owners troubled to go to a class and learnt to understand their dog and the correct way of controlling it.

Once the basic exercises of obedience and control have been learned most training societies encourage their members to go on and take part in competitions at shows. Success in obedience has always required a dog of balanced temperament, and an owner with patience and determination. To succeed with a Dobermann, noted for its initiative and quick reactions, means real dedication to the task and love of the breed. It is much easier to win competitions with the more submissive breeds of dog.

All classes of obedience tests at shows are run under K.C. rules.

A leaflet S(2) may be obtained from the Kennel Club (1–4 Clarges Street, Piccadilly, London W1Y 8AB) which gives the rules and definitions for obedience classes and full details of the exercises, their marking, etc. There are five separate classes of obedience tests, graduated upwards from beginners through novice, Test 'A' and Test 'B' to the open class Test 'C'. All classes include a stay exercise (where the dogs remain in sit or down position for a given length of time until rejoined by the handler), a retrieve (progressing from an article of the handler's choice to a dumb-bell and then to an article supplied by the judge), a recall (to sit in front or follow at heel) and heelwork (walking closely at handler's side on and off the lead). The higher grades of test include additional exercises: send away and drop on command, scent discrimination, etc. In the two lowest classes handlers may give extra commands or encouragement to their dogs; in Test 'C' only one command or a signal may be given, and all the exercises are carried out with the dog off the lead. A Kennel Club Obedience Certificate may be won by the best dog and the best bitch in Test 'C' at championship shows, provided a minimum of 290 out of 300 marks is obtained. A dog or bitch winning three obedience certificates under three different judges becomes an obedience champion. The number of championship shows with obedience certificates has increased steadily.

With emphasis on the trainability of this working breed, a few Dobermanns in the early days were professionally trained and handled. From the first litter bred by the Surrey Constabulary, the Chief Constable, the late Sir Joseph Simpson, K.B.E., K.P.M., presented a brown dog, Mountbrowne Joe, to the Dobermann Club for stud purposes. As the Kennel Club will not allow a dog registered in the name of a club to be shown either in breed or obedience classes or working trials Joe was transferred to Mrs. Mary Porterfield, who trained and handled him at all times. Following release from quarantine, Mrs. Julia Curnow's Prinses Anja v't Scheepjeskerk was trained by Audrey Montgomery and handled by her with great success during the summer of 1950. The Dobermann Club's Obedience Cup is awarded annually on points for each class won during the previous calendar year. The first holder was Prinses Anja, and Mountbrowne Joe won it in the following year. A son, daughter and grand-daughter of Prinses Anja have also won this trophy in later years.

Prinses Anja v't. Scheepjeskerk was the dam of Jupiter and Juno of Tavey. Jupiter became a breed champion at the age of fifteen months and then went to Bob Montgomery for training in obedience. At the same time Dennis and Philippa Thorne Dunn sent Juno to Audrey Montgomery, with whom she stayed for almost four months. During that time the wins of brother and sister were roughly parallel: at one show Jupiter was 1st and Juno 2nd in the novice class; a week later Juno was 2nd and Jupiter 3rd (and Juno won two breed classes at the same show). The following week at a championship obedience show, with the classes divided, Jupiter won novice dog and Juno won novice bitch. It is fascinating to speculate what might have happened had Juno been able to remain with Audrey Montgomery, but she returned to her owners and became a breed champion the following year.

At this point Bob Montgomery became the joint owner of Jupiter with Julia Curnow and handled him through all the grades of obedience tests. At his very first attempt in Test 'C' Jupiter won the class and the obedience certificate. For more than a year Jupiter was in Test 'C' at championship shows and was 2nd twice (and awarded reserve for the obedience certificate) and 3rd twice. In May 1955 he again won an obedience certificate and a month later added his third. So Jupiter of Tavey became an obedience champion as well as a breed champion. It is claimed that this double achievement is unique in the Dobermann breed.*
He was a deeply affectionate dog, completely honest and trustworthy, steady and loyal. Fortunately, he was used considerably for breeding and his qualities were maintained in individuals of succeeding generations. Several dogs well-known in obedience in their day had Ch. and Ob. Ch. Jupiter as their sire or grandsire.

There have been no other obedience champions in the breed. To date the nearest to the title has been Derek Tretheway's brown dog, Lionel of Rancliffe. A winner in every grade of tests, Lionel

* Mrs. Mary Warren of Kawerau, New Zealand, has a Dobermann bitch, N.Z. Ch. Alert Enchantress, who became a breed champion in 1967, qualified W.D. ex., U.D. ex. and C.D. ex. between 1968 and 1972 and became an Obedience Champion in 1971, all under New Zealand Kennel Club rules. This bitch holds the title of 'Dual Champion Alert Enchantress, C.D. ex., U.D. ex., W.D. ex.'.

reached the top and was campaigned steadily in the hottest championship competition during 1967 and 1968, winning four reserve and two obedience certificates. Another brown dog, Ian Inskip's Heiner Rustic, also won his way up to championship Test 'C' at this time and he won an obedience certificate in 1968.

The only other Dobermann to win an obedience certificate has been Terry Hadley's Yuba Adonis, a son of Ch. and Ob. Ch. Jupiter. His opportunities for competition were infrequent, but having reached Test 'C' in 1963 Yuba Adonis took a reserve certificate and a year later won his first obedience certificate. His owner did not continue in this type of competition, having greater interest in practical work. Yuba Adonis once searched and found a car key dropped in a ten-acre field and was frequently called in to help look for lost property. His owner had his own security business and says of his dog: 'I have earned my living with him over the past few years. He has a perfect temperament; can be handled by anyone when I am with him but would not back down for a lion. He has been put to the test many times with rough blokes who meant business. As a guard he is supreme.'

The breed champions Juno of Tavey and Tavey's Stormy Acacia worked in obedience competition before their top show successes. Both were trained and handled by Audrey Montgomery. Others who became champions were trained from the start both to work and show, and were handled by their owners in breed and obedience rings alike. After gaining their title they continued in obedience competition at local and club shows. The breed champions most successful in obedience, however, were Mrs. Margaret Bastable's Ch. Xel of Tavey and Harry Inskip's Ch. Tavey's Stormy Master, both of which graduated steadily through obedience and breed classes, and as breed champions both won in Test 'C' at big obedience shows.

Ch. Tumlow Whinlands Flurry was first owned by Mrs. Elizabeth Harris and in her hands became a breed champion in three successive shows. Transferred later to Mrs. Sheila Mitchell, Flurry became a family pet and for the first time lived in the house; she only started training on her fourth birthday. After so long in kennels Flurry had no idea of picking up any thrown article and it took nine months of patient work before she would retrieve, after which her progress was steady.

At club shows some notable family successes have been scored. In 1958, when competing in the same class, David Kingsberry's Brumbies Bandit was 1st, Brumbies Black Butterfly was 2nd, and their dam, Brumbies Black Baroness, was 4th. At the Midland Branch show in 1966 the litter-sisters Czarina and Edrika of Rhodesdobe, handled respectively by Lillian and Dudley Wontner-Smith, between them won four 1sts and three 2nds in four obedience classes.

At all-breed obedience shows, too, Dobermanns have sometimes taken the majority of prizes: at a show in the Midlands Jim Bramley's Delmordene Aster won beginners and novice with 100 per cent and 99 per cent marks and was 2nd in Test 'A' with 99 per cent of total marks, while Bryan Pole's Annastock Moonraker (Aster's sire) was 2nd in Test 'B' and 1st in Test 'C'. Some years earlier at a show in Scotland, where these were the only Dobermanns in obedience, Miss Betty Booker's Hussar of Skipwith won beginners and novice with 100 per cent and 99 per cent marks, and my own dogs Lorelei of Tavey won Test 'A' and Vyking Drum Major won Test 'B' and was 2nd in Test 'C'.

Besides the few mentioned there have been many other Dobermanns that proved very successful in open and championship obedience competition. It has unfortunately proved to be impossible to list them all, or to indicate the grades in which they attained success. The majority have been family dogs, trained and handled by their owners. Some never entered public competition, some competed for only one season and were then retired for breeding, others proved successful over a period of time.

The North of England and the Scottish Dobermann Club shows include obedience classes which are open to all breeds. These are supported by local training clubs, particularly those with a nucleus of members with Dobermanns. At the Dobermann Club and the Midland Club shows obedience classes are for Dobermanns only, and many taking part are shown in breed classes on the same day. The catalogues of club events in all areas show that breeding from the top sires and dams, whether of German or American origin, can successfully combine good conformation with intelligence and an aptitude for work. It is to be hoped that all-round ability will be maintained in the Dobermann breed.

9
Working Trials

In the *Kennel Club Stud Book* of 1953 are the names of the first Dobermanns to gain entry by reason of wins in breed classes at shows. The working potential of the breed had, however, already hit the headlines and attracted interest. For three years Dobermanns had won recognition and Stud Book entry through their achievements in championship working trials.

These events are run under Kennel Club rules, the various stakes scheduled covering either one or two days of tests. The stakes are competitive in that prizes are given to the first three dogs in each grade, but the chief attraction for competitors is that a certificate of qualification is awarded to every dog that obtains the requisite percentage of total marks allotted to the stake. The top working qualifications of 'Police Dog' (P.D.) and 'Tracking Dog' (T.D.) are officially added to the registered name of the dog by the Kennel Club in its records and registers. It is, however, customary for the owners of dogs that have qualified in any working trials stake to add the grade of qualification obtained when quoting the dog's name on a pedigree or entry form. This unofficial practice has not been censured. Qualification has never been easy, and graduation through the different stakes is recognised in the dog world as proof of the ability desirable in any working breed.

The schedule of working trials stakes remained almost unchanged from their post-war resumption in 1947 until the end of 1960. The Junior Stakes carried no qualification but served as an introduction to trials for those dogs already trained for obedience competition. The other one-day stakes officially called 'Senior B' were better known as the 'Companion Dog Stakes' since this was the qualification awarded to dogs passing the required tests of general obedience and agility. The first of the two-day trials stakes was called 'Senior A', more generally known as the 'Utility Dog Stakes'. The tracking and seek-back took place in open country one day, and the general obedience and agility on the second day. From 1955 a dog had to qualify 'U.D.ex.' before being allowed to enter the Open Stakes. There have always been two separate and different Open Stakes: one Police Dog, the other Tracking Dog Stakes. In both, the tracking took place on the first day and the general obedience and agility on the second. The Defence Work section of the Police Dog Stakes followed the general obedience on the second day. Under Kennel Club Working Trials Rules the winner in the Open Stakes at a championship trials was awarded a working trials certificate provided at least 80 per cent of maximum points had been secured. Two such working trials certificates under two different judges entitled a dog to become a working trials champion.

During the 1950s interest in dog-training increased steadily throughout the country, the standard of general obedience be-came higher, and more civilian handlers came into working trials competition. When the police had their own regional and national trials fewer were entered in working trials under Kennel Club rules. To meet this changing situation three members of the K.C. Working Trials Council—Mr. R. Matchell and Mr. R. M. Montgomery with the late Sir Joseph Simpson in the chair—were appointed to consider revision of the schedule. They com-bined the widest possible experience of training and handling dogs of different breeds, and of organising and judging working trials. Their recommendations were in due course approved and passed through all stages at the Kennel Club. The revised working trials schedule, which became operative on 1st January 1961, has con-tinued in the same general form until now.

The Junior Stakes were abolished. The Companion Dog Stake was still a one-day event with tests of general obedience and agility, some in a modified form. In the renamed Utility Dog Qualifying Stake the jumps in the agility section were now com-pulsorily of maximum size and a dog was still required to qualify 'U.D.ex.' before being allowed to enter the Open Stakes. A new

Koriston Pewter Strike of Doberean, T.D. ex, W.D. ex, U.D. ex,
C.D. ex, in action

Sally Anne Thompson

Training for manwork

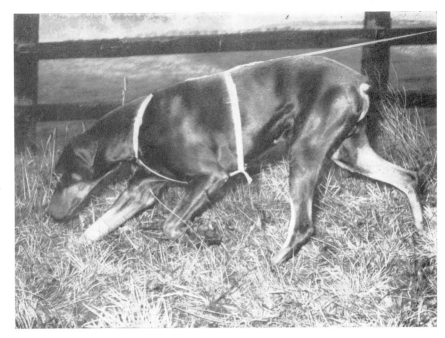

Ch. Tavey's Stormy Acacia in tracking harness

Herald Photographic Service.

Training with the dumb-bell

Chandlers of Exeter

Mr. J. Carpenter with his guide-dog   Trudi of Ely demonstrates a soft mouth

Dollar Premium, T.D. ex, W.D. ex, U.D. ex, C.D. ex.

The difference between cropped and normal eared Dobermanns is exemplified by these two head studies.

The bitch with that lovely glint in her eyes is Ch. Royaltains Babette of Tavey, winner of six Challenge Certificates

American-bred bitch Arawak Perfecta, imported by Mrs. Curnow in 1972 and greatly admired for her beauty, temperament and character

stake of equivalent category was introduced, called the All Breeds Working Dog Stake. In this stake the size of the jumps varied according to the size of the dog. This enabled smaller dogs to qualify in a two-day stake, but 'W.D.ex' did not allow them to enter the Open Stakes. The Utility Dog was the Qualifying Stake until the end of 1966. The exercises of general obedience in the Open Stakes were reduced in number and greater emphasis was placed on the specialised tests relevant either to a police dog or a tracking dog. The conditions for gaining a Working Trials certificate remained the same.

The most important change was in the grouping of exercises in each stake according to their type: Heelwork (separate in C.D. only), Control, Agility, Tracking, Search, Patrol (P.D. only). The marks for each exercise were greatly reduced and the group total marks now became the vital factor in the final reckoning for a qualification. No dog could qualify unless it obtained 70 per cent or more marks in each group. The added qualification of 'Excellent' still required at least 80 per cent of the possible total marks for the stake. By these requirements the overall standard of performance at working trials was immediately raised. From 1961 on qualification in any stake became more difficult and was a real test of all-round ability, for the new system of marking allowed only a small margin of error and an otherwise brilliant dog could forfeit qualification by failure in just one exercise.

In this revised and challenging form the schedule still operates today, with one important amendment which came into force on 1st January 1967. With ever-greater interest in trials there had by then been a steady build-up of entries in the Open Stakes by dogs qualified 'U.D.ex.' but not yet up to the standard required for a P.D. or a T.D. qualification. The Open Stakes were increasingly overcrowded with a considerable proportion of the dogs still too inexperienced to have any chance of qualifying. The Working Dog Stake was therefore upgraded by raising the tracking requirements and making the jumps in the agility group compulsorily of maximum height. The Utility Dog Stake—renamed the All Breeds Utility Dog Stake and with jumps now varied according to the size of the dog—became the first in a two-stage graduation. A dog was now required to qualify 'U.D.ex.' and then 'W.D.ex.'

E

before being allowed to enter the Open Stakes. The Working Dog became the Qualifying Stake, and the position is the same today.

A leaflet S(1) may be obtained from the Kennel Club (1–4 Clarges Street, Piccadilly, London W1Y 8AB) which gives the rules and regulations currently in force for working trials, together with full details of the stakes, conduct of each exercise, their marking, etc.

In the U.S.A. and in Canada apparently similar qualifications (CD, CDX, UD, TD, TDX) may be gained by pure-bred dogs trained for 'obedience trials' and 'tracking tests' held under the rules of the American and Canadian Kennel Clubs. The titles 'Tracking Dog' (TD) and 'Tracking Dog Excellent' (TDX) are awarded to dogs that have successfully worked a Leash Track of approximately the same standard as those of the British Utility Dog and Tracking Dog Stakes respectively. They certainly prove aptitude and ability in tracking, but the tracking tests in both North American countries are organised as a separate activity and are confined to a leash track only. The qualifications CD, CDX and UD may be gained by pure-bred dogs trained for obedience trials; the exercises in each of these grades more closely resemble those of the obedience classes at shows in the United Kingdom than the British working trials. Obedience trials take place at both indoor and outdoor shows, a high average pass-mark is required, and a dog must pass three times under three different judges before being granted a certificate and permitted to use the appropriate letters after its name, but the exercises of obedience and control in America and Canada are fewer in number and appear to be more limited in scope than in the British working trials. The maximum size of the jumps in the higher grades is considerably less than in our schedule, and the nosework is confined to tests of scent discrimination (and in Canada a seek-back as well), very much as in our obedience classes. The American and Canadian CD, CDX and UD titles resulting from their obedience trials are not comparable to the C.D., C.D.ex. or U.D. qualifications gained by the Dobermanns mentioned in this account of working trials in the U.K. Their TD and TDX titles are proof of a standard of proficiency in tracking equivalent to British U.D. and T.D. qualified dogs, but are considered a specialist activity and are not gained in association with any other kind of tests.

In the United Kingdom the number of working trials certificates available each year is controlled by the Kennel Club, allocation being dependent upon the support given to working trials in the previous years and upon the status of the organising body. Up to the end of 1954 the only society running championship working trials was the Associated Sheep, Police and Army Dog Society, known as 'A.S.P.A.D.S.'. Originally an Alsatian breed club putting on a championship breed show each year, membership had been opened to owners of all breeds of dog. It was the Society's policy to run working trials with the local organisation based upon the nearest A.S.P.A.D.S. branch, of which between ten and twenty existed in all parts of the country up to the middle of the 1950s. Each branch held a weekly obedience-training class for dogs of all breeds. In time the A.S.P.A.D.S. branch organisations formed the nucleus of many of the best independent training societies in existence today. From a single working trials meeting in 1947, records show two A.S.P.A.D.S. trials held in 1948 (one with Police Dog, the other with Tracking Dog Open Stakes), three in 1949 and four annually from 1950 to 1954, with the Open Stakes alternately Police Dog and Tracking Dog.

Before Dobermanns were imported or trained in the U.K., Harry Darbyshire was competing in working trials with his own Alsatians, which won and qualified in the various stakes. Sir Joseph Simpson and his wife also supported working trials with their Labradors. It was therefore not surprising that this mutual interest should be continued after Sir Joseph had become Chief Constable of Surrey and Harry Darbyshire was appointed by him sergeant in charge of the dog section. Police dog-handlers trained at constabulary headquarters at Mountbrowne, Guildford, were encouraged to enter and qualify their dogs in working trials.

The first Dobermann to do so was the Surrey Constabulary's Ulf v. Margarethenhof. At trials in June 1949 he was entered in three stakes. At that time entry in any of the lower stakes was restricted only by reason of previous wins in higher grades and the Open Stakes were open to all. In two days of tests Ulf v. Margarethenhof won a place in each stake. He qualified C.D.ex., U.D.ex., P.D.ex., and was the winner of the Open Stakes and of his first working trials certificate, a spectacular debut for the breed.

Entered in the Open Stakes at subsequent trials during the next fourteen months Ulf was either 2nd or 3rd on each occasion and added T.D.ex. to his other qualifications. In July 1950 he again won the Police Dog Stake and his 2nd working trials certificate and became the breed's first working trials champion.

Having gained his title Ulf v. Margarethenhof was not entered again in working trials. His ability was, however, inherited by successive generations of Dobermanns in police service. His influence on the working side was equalled only by Donathe v. Begertal, foundation bitch of the Mountbrowne line. In the classified list of qualifiers in Appendix G it can be seen that every one of the Dobermanns bred by the police traces back to Donathe v. Begertal; all but two have Ulf v. Margarethenhof as their sire or grandsire. The two dogs and three bitches from their first litter all qualified U.D.ex. (and four qualified C.D.ex. as well) before they were two years old. Of these Mountbrowne Juno and Mountbrowne Justice were not entered in trials again. The others were prizewinners in every stake in which they qualified and all of them won a working trials certificate. Mountbrowne Jenny won the Tracking Dog Stake and a certificate in 1952. Tipped to become the breed's next working trials champion this brilliant little bitch contracted hardpad and died before she was three years old. Mountbrowne Joe in civilian hands won a Police Dog Stake and a certificate in 1953. Mountbrowne Julie won the Open Stakes three times and became a working trials champion in 1955. From Donathe v. Begertal's second litter Mountbrowne Karen was retained for duty with the Surrey Constabulary, and in 1955 she, too, became a working trials champion.

The three brown Dobermanns bred by the Durham Constabulary from Mountbrowne Julie were also prizewinners in the Open Stakes where they excelled in manwork. Indeed it was their keenness—and consequent failure to recall from the running criminal without a bite—that cost them the top award time after time. One of them, Joseph of Aycliffe, did become a working trials champion like his dam and grandsire. It is believed that a comparable standard of achievement in three successive generations has not been equalled in a working breed.

Joseph's sister, Jenny of Ayclifden, was mated to her famous

grandsire, W.T. Ch. Ulf v. Margarethenhof. The resulting litter
of eight puppies when they were fully grown passed out successfully from their basic and advanced courses of training as police
dogs and all were retained for service in the county. It is rare to
achieve 100 per cent success in temperament and ability with
every member of a litter of this size. In championship working
trials two of them—Arno of Aycliffe and Anna of Aycliffe—won a
working trials certificate, and Alouette and Asta of Aycliffe both
qualified in lower stakes.

Members of later litters of police-bred Dobermanns had fewer
opportunities for competition in working trials. When entered
they qualified well. Mountbrowne Yukon and Mountbrowne
Astor excelled in tracking ability. Mountbrowne Amber, fresh
from a course of advanced training, won both trials stakes in which
she was entered in 1957 and, later, she qualified in both Open
Stakes.

Such successes in trials were not cheaply won. Although there
were fewer entries then than now, there were more exercises to
be carried out in each stake and twelve months could elapse before
there was an opportunity to enter a dog again. Police dogs,
whether Dobermanns or Alsatians, were in public competition
against civilian Alsatians and Labradors handled by men and
women with many years' experience of training. The standard of
the day was high.

Dobermanns in police service were, of course, selected and bred
for working ability. Civilian stock was assessed primarily for conformation and show potential but did not thereby necessarily
lack ability. Selection was made from original stock with intelligence and good temperament. Dobermanns bred from dogs and
bitches imported by private owners made the grade when trained
for working trials, although in number they were relatively few.

The first civilian Dobermanns entered in working trials were
trained by professional handlers. Mountbrowne Joe has already
been mentioned; his owner Mary Porterfield ranked as a profe-
sional handler because of her other work with dogs. Bob and
Audrey Montgomery were professional trainers of all types of
dogs. In their hands, and after only a limited time for training,
Vyking Don of Tavey was a prizewinner in Junior Stakes in 1950

and Prinses Anja v't Scheepjeskerk qualified C.D.ex. and U.D. in 1951. Bob Montgomery became joint-owner with the breeder of Ch. and Ob. Ch. Jupiter of Tavey. With him Jupiter qualified C.D.ex. and won the Junior Stakes at trials in 1953.

No training courses were available then for civilian handlers wanting to train their own dogs. The exercises of basic obedience and control were learned at local all-breed training classes, a scale jump was either improvised or practised occasionally when visiting a friend with such equipment. Sound advice on the mysteries of tracking could rarely be obtained and then, generally, only from a handler with an understanding of other breeds. Experience was gained from watching trials and talking to the police handlers, and then by having a go and learning through failure and success.

Other than Mountbrowne Joe the first owner-handled Dobermann to qualify was Vyking Drum Major, a son of Vyking Don of Tavey. Entered in trials during his owner's annual holiday he qualified C.D.ex. in 1951, won the stake when qualifying U.D.ex. in 1953, was 2nd in the Tracking Dog Open Stakes when Mountbrowne Kareñ was the winner in 1954, and qualified P.D. in 1956.

David Kingsberry first came into working trials in 1955 with his bitch Brumbies Black Baroness. She qualified U.D.ex. and was twice a prizewinner in the C.D. stakes when she qualified 'excellent'. Her son Brumbies Bandit was also twice a prizewinner when qualifying in the C.D. stakes.

Lorelei of Tavey, a daughter of Prinses Anja v't. Scheepjeskerk, was selected for show and working potential. At her annual outing to a championship show she took three reserve best bitch awards and one challenge certificate; she won first prizes in breed and obedience classes and working trials alike over a period of three years. She was 2nd in both the C.D. and the U.D. Stakes, then won the U.D. Stake four times and was the first civilian Dobermann bitch to qualify T.D.ex.

No list of names such as appears in the Appendix can convey the tension and excitement that often accompanied wins and qualifications in working trials. In 1951, when Donathe v. Begertal won both stakes in which she was entered, two of her daughters were in 2nd and 3rd place. Later that year Mountbrowne Joe, Mountbrowne Jenny and Prinses Anja v't Scheepjeskerk were in

2nd, 3rd and 4th places when qualifying in the same stake. Study of marked catalogues shows that sometimes the Dobermanns that took top placings were the only representatives of their breed in the stake.

Such, however, was not the case in 1956. A well-known manufacturer of dog foods had presented to the A.S.P.A.D.S. the Carta Carna Challenge Cup for the best working police dog in the country. The annual contest for this trophy was the P.D. Open Stakes at the summer meeting. In 1956 it was on offer at A.S.P.A.D.S. trials held in the Darlington area, with local organisation in the hands of the Durham Constabulary. In the Open Stakes four out of ten police dogs were Dobermanns. The U.D. and C.D. stakes had the largest entry to date with thirty-three and thirty-four respectively. Ten out of nineteen police dogs in the U.D. stake were Dobermanns. The results were as spectacular as was the entry. The winner of the Open Stakes was Joseph of Aycliffe, who qualified and won his first working trials certificate and the Carta Carna Cup for the 'Police Dog of the Year'. In 2nd and 3rd place behind him came W.T. Ch. Mountbrowne Karen and Jenny of Ayclifden. These three Dobermanns were the only dogs in the stake to qualify 'excellent'. Competition in the Utility Dog stake was neck-and-neck until the final exercise, when Lorelei of Tavey won, with Mountbrowne Olaf 2nd and Mountbrowne Pluto in 4th place. Brumbies Black Baroness was 2nd in the Companion Dog Stake. Neither before nor since have so many Dobermanns taken part in one event.

The officers in some police forces considered that participation in trials under Kennel Club rules had no value for a police dog. They therefore welcomed the introduction in 1958 of annual trials for police dogs organised on the authority of the Home Office. These were open to handlers representing every force with a dog section. The national entry at first was judged within a week. After a few years the increase in numbers led to trials being held first in different regions, the two leading dogs from each regional trials competing later in the National Police Dog Trials. The availability of their own special trials tended to diminish police support for working trials under Kennel Club rules.

At the same time a steadily increasing demand for working

trials events was coming from the civilian handlers of Alsatians, Border Collies, Boxers and Labradors. Licence to hold trials was therefore gradually extended by the Kennel Club to other societies with an interest in training. In 1955, the A.S.P.A.D.S.' allotment was raised to five championship meetings and their annual share has been maintained at this figure to the present day. The total number of working trials championships was increased to six in 1955, seven in 1957, nine in 1958, and ten in 1960. Increased support for working trials was not, however, given by many owners of Dobermanns at this time. Besides David Kingsberry and myself with dogs already mentioned, the only civilian handlers to come into trials were Derek Lee, whose Eclipse of Tavey qualified C.D.ex. in 1959, and Betty Booker, whose Hussar of Skipwith was successful in the Junior Stakes a year or two earlier. Otherwise, interest in the breed at this time was concentrated on the show possibilities and not on the working side.

When the revised schedule of working trials became operative in 1961 there were few Dobermanns left in police service. Replacements were bred by the Durham Constabulary from later imported stock, but none of them has ever been entered in civilian trials. For a year or two police dogs that added to the qualifications they had already gained under the old schedule included Arno of Aycliffe, Mountbrowne Amber, Mountbrowne Yukon and Bowesmoor Gina. Police dogs new to trials that qualified under the 1961 schedule were Faust of Cartergate, Flame and Fangio of Aycliffe, Bowesmoor Herma, Goliath of Dissington and Mountbrowne Barry. Flame of Aycliffe and Faust of Cartergate were both winners of the stake when they qualified U.D.ex.

With the phasing out of the Dobermann as a police dog a compensating interest in the working side of the breed developed in the early 1960s among civilian owners. Some acquired their Dobermann for its training possibilities, others found a challenge in training a show dog whose immediate forbears were unproved in tests or trials. Colin Brockett and Ian Stewart came into trials at this time and over three or four years their Dobermanns graduated steadily through to qualifications in an Open Stake. Maverick the Brave was the first of his breed to qualify P.D.ex. under the new schedule and Barnard of Caedan the first to qualify

T.D.ex. My Doberean Patience followed family tradition on her dam's side by dual success in breed competition and working trials. She won the Utility Dog stake within weeks of an award of reserve best bitch at a championship show and on other occasions was a prizewinner equally in trials and shows.

In 1963 the total number of championship working trials was increased to twelve and the Dobermann breed was represented at most of them. At one trials in the Midlands the winner of the Utility Dog stake was Bracken of Cartergate; of thirty-one dogs entered in the Companion Dog stake on the same occasion 5 were Dobermanns and all of them qualified C.D.ex. Among them was Hawk of Trevellis, qualifying in the first stage of what proved to be a very successful career in working trials. Bernard Horton and his wife had bred Hawk; Bernard trained and handled him year by year through C.D.ex. and U.D.ex. into the Open Stake, where Hawk was 4th in the Tracking Dog Stake but failed to qualify on that occasion. After Bernard's death Hawk passed into the ownership of Harry Appleby, an experienced handler and a friend of Bernard's. With him Hawk won the Tracking Dog Open Stake in 1966, qualifying T.D.ex. and gaining a working trials certificate, the first civilian-bred Dobermann ever to achieve this. A year later Hawk qualified P.D.ex. and so completed the total of working trials qualifications open to him.

Yuba Adonis, a son of Ch. and Ob.Ch. Jupiter of Tavey, had already won an obedience certificate when he came into working trials in 1965. He qualified C.D.ex. and U.D.ex. and added P.D.ex. in 1967. Like Hawk of Trevellis, Yuba Adonis was a good-looking dog that won in breed classes when shown as a junior. Another regular winner in top obedience competition and the holder of an obedience certificate was Heiner Rustic, who qualified C.D.ex. at least twice and won the stake.

Dandy of Dovecote was a Dobermann of great ability. He won a place in every stake in which he qualified during three seasons of trials. He was the winner of the Utility Dog Stake in 1966, qualified T.D.ex. a few weeks later, was winner of the Working Dog Stake in 1967 when it became the qualifier for entry into the Open, and was 2nd and the best civilian dog in a Tracking Dog Stake in 1968 when he qualified 'excellent'.

Bowesmoor Otis met her owner and handler by mere chance. Her original owners were unable to keep her and took her to be destroyed. In the waiting-room at the veterinary surgeon's they met Jim Whytock, who had just had his old Labrador put to sleep. He took over Bowesmoor Otis, trained her for trials and she qualified U.D.ex. in 1965. She was entered in trials several times later and gained high marks in nosework, but she never liked the scale jump and forfeited further qualification through failure of this exercise.

The only breed champion trained for working trials since Jupiter of Tavey eleven years previously was Ch. Wyndenhelms AWOL. Throughout her show and working career she was trained and handled by her owner, George Thompson. She qualified in two stakes in 1964, coming equal 2nd in the Utility Dog.

Three young Dobermanns already successful in the show ring became prizewinners in working trials as they graduated through into the Open Stakes. Dollar Premium qualified well in each stage, C.D.ex., U.D.ex. and W.D.ex. At his first attempt in an Open Stake he won the trophy for the best T.D. track, but failed to qualify; in 1968 he successfully added T.D.ex. to his other qualifications. Gurnard Gloomy Sunday and Tavey's Stormy Jael both qualified C.D.ex. and U.D.ex. before they were two years old. Gurnard Gloomy Sunday won the Utility Dog Stake in 1967 and was 4th in the Tracking Dog Open Stake when he qualified 'excellent'. Tavey's Stormy Jael was 3rd in the Working Dog Stake in 1967 but failed to qualify. Two months later she qualified T.D.ex., the first Dobermann bitch to do so under the 1961 schedule and only the second civilian bitch of her breed ever to qualify in an Open Stake.

From 1967 the annual total of fourteen championship working trials has been maintained, with trials being run by seven different societies to date. The overall standard of performance required to qualify in any stake under the present schedule is higher than it was when the early Dobermanns qualified, but comparison cannot properly be made as in earlier years the conditions and opportunities both for training and competition were so different. In those days handlers worked very much on their own; failure in competition showed up weakness and faults, success confirmed training was on the right lines. Opportunity for entering trials might then come only once a year, or twice if one was lucky. Since the introduction of the new schedule, training for trials has sometimes been arranged for small groups working under the supervision of a police handler. Those with former experience of Dobermanns in police service have always given encouragement and advice to civilian handlers. At training classes organised by clubs in different areas instruction in the various jumps is increasingly included and tracking practice arranged during the summer months. The original way of learning how to train and handle a lively intelligent Dobermann through trial and error takes too long; qualification in either of the Open Stakes at working trials can be obtained now only after many months of specialised training and a long programme of graduation through the lower stakes. Indeed, in 1969 this was extended even further; no dog may now enter either the Utility or Working Dog Stake at championship trials until it has previously obtained a certificate of merit in the same stake at an open trials. This certificate of merit carries only the right to enter at a championship event. It does not bestow qualification in the stake concerned, which as before can be obtained only at championship trials. In 1975 graduation was extended one step further: a certificate of merit is required as well in the Tracking Dog Stake at an open trials. Thus any dog aspiring to enter the Tracking Dog Stake at championship trials must already hold certificates of merit (with 80% total marks) from open trials in Utility, Working and Tracking Dog grades plus U.D.ex. and W.D.ex. championship trials qualifications.

A list of Dobermanns that have qualified in two-day stakes (i.e. those involving tracking as well as the general obedience and agility tests) is given in Appendix G. Unfortunately, space does not permit inclusion of those dogs and bitches that qualified 'C.D.' only or which before 1961 were winners in the Junior Stakes. The list has been compiled from information supplied by the owners and handlers of the dogs concerned and from study of catalogues, trials reports and Kennel Club Stud Books. It does not claim to be complete but may at least give an idea of the working potential and ability of the breed.

10

Dobermann Club Working Tests

IN Germany a working qualification is not required before a Dobermann can gain the title of Sieger or Siegerin; the Dobermann Verein does, however, encourage its members to qualify their show stock in the working field. Most of the German forbears of the dogs and bitches originally imported carried working qualifications and at first the type of Dobermann bred in this country was similar. After a decade of breeding and the consequent expansion in numbers some people felt it would be a good thing if owners could have an opportunity of proving their dog was still capable of working in the traditional way. The committee of the Dobermann Club has always included those who admire the breed for its ability as well as its appearance, and they supported the idea. A copy of the German tests for the breed was obtained and translated. A sub-committee of members with experience of training and handling was appointed to draw up tests suitable for Dobermanns in U.K. and two meetings took place in the winter of 1960–1.

While adhering to the basic pattern of the German tests it was agreed to consider amendment where any exercise might cause confusion to a dog already trained for obedience or working trials, or where they seemed inappropriate to the role of the civilian Dobermann in Britain. In Germany, Dobermanns are kept primarily as working dogs and are considered guards but with aptitude for nosework. They are required to show courage and be resolute in manwork and to prove they are obedient and under control. In the show ring they are tested for temperament (reacting to a threat while being restrained on the leash), and conformation is assessed by the judge walking round and making visual examina-

tion. In Britain, Dobermanns in the show ring must allow themselves to be handled. In their home life as family dogs they are
required to be alert and courageous, but the training of civilian
dogs for manwork is considered undesirable except in the hands
of an expert. The emphasis on guarding, defence and attack in
each grade of the German tests did not therefore seem suitable for
Dobermanns in Britain.

The German working tests consisted of 'Dobermann Tests I,
II and III' and a 'Dobermann Tracking Test'. Tests I, II and III
were all of similar pattern and were divided into sections: 'Scent
Performance', 'General Obedience', and 'Guarding and Defence'.
A few of the individual exercises were described in very great
detail, others were given in terms so general that they were open
to wide variations of interpretation. The working tests for
British Dobermanns are the same in number but have been drawn
up with a different emphasis at each stage.

Test I has three sections. The leash-track laid by the handler
twenty minutes previously has two turns and an article at the end.
General obedience is covered by seven exercises: heel on lead
(passing through and standing among a small group of people as
well as the usual turns, halts, and changes of pace), heel free (with
a test of steadiness to gun-shots), drop on command and recall,
retrieve (of dumb-bell or article of handler's choice), stand for
examination (the dog allowing itself to be handled as if at a show),
the down exercise (staying down five minutes with the handler in
sight) and a clear jump over a 3 ft hurdle. The section originally
headed 'Guarding and Defence' was later changed to 'Test of
Courage', but otherwise is as in the German version of the tests,
which specifies a sudden threat by a mock attacker as the handler
walks by with his dog on the lead. It is in a situation such as this
in everyday life when a Dobermann should react in defence of his
owner, either by standing his ground or going forward to challenge the stranger, or by barking to deter him. Courage must be
shown and the instinct to defend his owner should be inherent in
the breed. The inclusion of this Section in this form has been
strongly criticised subsequently, in the context that it is an incite-
ment to owners to teach their dogs to bite and become aggressive.
The members of the 1960 sub-committee still hold to their views

in full support of this test, and no objection has ever been made by any of the judges approved by the Dobermann Club to officiate at these working tests. No biting or manwork is necessary and aggression is not required. The dog when out for a walk with its owner is merely required to show that it is prepared to react like a Dobermann, i.e. with courage. A dog that is aggressive and ready to bite is to be discouraged as much as one that jumps back and retreats behind its owner. A pass-mark in all three sections of Test I is compulsory before attempting a higher grade.

Test II covers more advanced nosework and general obedience and is aimed at encouraging handlers to train their dogs to a standard beyond that of the basic Test I. Scent performance includes a controlled search for four articles (the dog working within an area approximately twenty-five yards each way) and the leash-track is one hour old, with four articles and four turns. Under general obedience the exercises of heel on lead, heel free, drop on command and retrieve are repeated from the earlier test except that the retrieve article is provided by the judge. Additional exercises in this section are the send away, speak on command, retrieve over a 3 ft hurdle and the standard tests of agility: 6 ft scale jump and 9 ft long jump. It requires a well-trained dog with steadiness and ability to pass this test with the required minimum of 70 per cent of total marks (at least 50 per cent in each section), but is still within the scope of a civilian handler with an interest in working trials.*

Having successfully passed Tests I and II either of the two remaining tests may be attempted; one is suitable for a fully-trained police dog, the other is a tracking test of a high standard. In Test III the leash track is half a mile long, thirty minutes old with three articles. Instead of repeating the full range of exercises in general obedience there is heel free (with complete indifference by the dog to pistol shots), a send away of at least fifty yards with a redirection to another given place, the down exercise (the handler being out of sight for ten minutes) and controlled jumping. This last exercise is included in trials for police dogs, when the handler walks past a line of jumps—four hurdles, a 9 ft long jump, and a 6 ft scale jump—and the dog at his command clears each obstacle

---

*Increasing support by members in the 1970s showed the need for an intermediate grade between tests I and II; so in Sept. 1978 test IA was introduced.

in turn. **Defence Work,** the third section of this test, corresponds to the standard required of a British police dog on completion of its advanced training course. It consists of four separate exercises: location of criminal by the dog quartering and searching; escort of criminal; escape prevention (by the dog holding fast and leaving automatically when resistance ceases), and a test of courage. In this, the handler having been incapacitated, the dog must of his own accord give chase to the escaping running criminal and when threatened by him detain the man by circling or biting him.

The final test has been renamed the Advanced Tracking Test. It may be attempted once Test II has been passed. The length of the leash-track that is the sole exercise of this test has been in-increased to one mile and it must be laid over varying terrain. The German version of this test had three cross-tracks introduced at precise places but these have been omitted as, with a time lapse of three hours before the track is run, some interference inevitably occurs at one point or another. A pass in this tracking test can be achieved only by a dog of considerable experience and tracking ability.

Copies of the working tests, together with details of procedure and marking, were distributed to all members of the Dobermann Club and were adopted at the Annual General Meeting in March 1961.

The first tests were held in the summer of that year. Harry Darbyshire judged and there was a good attendance of members watching the proceedings and learning from his comments and advice. The tracks were laid and run in fields adjacent to the sports ground where the general obedience took place, so everybody could see exactly what each dog did. The test of courage also took place in full view of the spectators; each handler and dog walked towards a belt of trees, where they were confronted by a man who stepped out in front of them with his arm raised, holding a rolled-up newspaper. No word was given to the dog (the judge had in-structed each handler to go for a walk without any warning to the dog as to what might happen), and as the handler advanced fur-ther towards the man he waved his newspaper threateningly and shouted at them. The reaction of dog and handler was carefully noted by the judge, and after an argument the man turned away and handler and dog walked back to the pavilion. A short while later, as they stood quietly near the spectators, the judge walked by with a short stick in one hand and an old mackintosh over the other arm. As he passed in front of the handler he shouted and raised the stick. When the dog moved forward, or barked, the raincoat was flapped quickly in its face. To the younger dogs this was totally unexpected (as the judge meant it to be) and they jumped back and then went forward with even greater determination, barking more loudly.

All the dogs in Test I that day were being judged by a top trainer of police dogs who had full knowledge of the way dogs are tested in Germany, but clearly his interpretation of the test of courage was in accord with those responsible for drawing up the tests, and no aggression or biting was required. The men who shouted and confronted the handler with a rolled newspaper or stick and flapping coat could have been eccentric people met by chance any day, and the reaction of the Dobermanns had to be courageous and determined but not vicious. It was again stressed that a family dog taught to bite becomes a liability and that man-work should be reserved for specialist working dogs in the hands of an expert.

In the next three years working tests were included in the pro-gramme of the Summer Rally of the Dobermann Club. The track-ing took place in the morning on suitable land nearby, and the remaining tests in the afternoon in the grounds of the home of whichever member of the club was host or hostess for the occasion. The Club Rally is principally a social affair to which all members and their Dobermanns are invited, but they are en-couraged to be participants as well as spectators of the various activities arranged, the programme being varied each year but always including events for show exhibitors and for those who enjoy working their dogs. The holding of the club working tests in conjunction with the rally was a very good way of bringing together members with different interests in the same breed, and the purpose of the working tests was fulfilled when the same dog or bitch combined good conformation and working ability and was seen to take part in both types of activity. In those days the owners came from widely separated parts of the country, having worked on their own to train their dogs to track and search and jump, and they enjoyed both the social and the working aspects and the atmosphere of a club occasion.

In 1965 the Dobermann Club appointed a sub-committee of six members to run the working tests, under the chairmanship of Rex Hodge. It takes considerable organisation to find enough suitable open country that is available for tracking, with an enclosed area of level ground for the jumps, general obedience and other exercises. Some competitors travel a long way to have their dogs tested, the judges generally give up their free day to officiate and stewards are needed to lay tracks and act as attackers. The judges have been either police officers who have themselves handled a Dobermann in police service, or civilians whose dogs have passed at least two of the working tests. During the 1970s other and newer members have come forward to serve on the sub-committee in their turn, and have worked with enthusiasm to maintain interest in the working side. Tests have been organised in the northwest as well as in the south of England, and this has enabled a greater number of club members than before to take part. Since 1975 new judges have been brought in, all of them experienced in handling working dogs but not necessarily Dobermanns.

Appendix H gives details of those Dobermanns that have successfully passed one or more of the club's working tests since their inauguration nineteen years ago. Tests have been held generally twice a year. Some of the dogs that have failed at their first attempt have passed at a later date. It has always been recognised that a club diploma for a pass in any test is not easily won. The schedule has been found adequate for assessing ability, nosework potential, agility, obedience, courage and steadiness of temperament. The conduct of the tests has always been strictly controlled by the Dobermann Club and entry is confined to its members, in order that there shall be no distortion of their purpose and no lowering of the standard required for a pass. The record to date has proved the wisdom of this policy and has shown that a Dobermann bred from sound stock can still rightly be classed a working dog. Indeed in 1977 and 1978 three Breed Champions were among the sixteen new names added to the roll of those successful in working tests.

11

Dobermanns in Police Service

WHEN the late Sir Joseph Simpson, K.B.E., K.P.M., became Chief
Constable of Surrey he initiated the formation of a dog section.
Besides Alsatians of the best working type, two Dobermanns were
selected in Germany and imported in September 1948. They entered police service on 1st March 1949. They were a brown dog,
Astor v.d. Morgensonne, and a black-and-tan bitch, Donathe v.
Begertal. At the same time, a black-and-tan dog, Ulf v. Margarethenhof, was taken over by Harry Darbyshire and joined the dog
section at constabulary headquarters at Mountbrowne, Guildford.
This dog had been brought over from Germany by an American
and after release from quarantine was found to be unmanageable
and out of control.

The policy laid down in Surrey at that time has formed the basis
of present-day policy and the ever-widening use of police dogs.
Although for more than ten years now the Alsatian has been the
breed officially recommended as being the most suitable for police
work, in the early days Dobermann and Alsatian litters were bred
at Mountbrowne in roughly equal numbers. Between January
1950 and November 1955 ten Dobermann litters are recorded.
Handlers came from various county forces, took over their particular dog when it was about ten months old and stayed for pre-
liminary training at Mountbrowne. After a few months back in
their own area they returned to Surrey for an advanced training
course.

Donathe v. Begertal had three litters. Being frequently under
pressure to use the Surrey police dogs for breeding with civilian
stock, Sir Joseph Simpson presented the brown dog, Mountbrowne Joe, to the Dobermann Club for stud purposes. Joe was

kept at the Bowesmoor kennels by Mary Porterfield and was trained and handled by her.

Ulf v. Margarethenhof and Astor v.d. Morgensonne were both used in regular police work in Surrey. Ulf was trained by Harry Darbyshire, who handled him in working trials (where he became the breed's first working trials champion) and in all his most important police work. Anyone who knew Ulf will still remember his tremendous tracking ability, his zest for work and his enthusiasm and speed in manwork. He had a passion for firearms and was so quick to 'go in' at the firing of a shot that his face was often singed by the powder. This led to his being used in cases involving searching for weapons and in following up dangerous men known to be violent or armed, besides normal police-dog duty. The following are the only two cases which still remain in the records at the Mountbrowne Kennels.

In December 1949 a child of eight years old was reported missing. The weather was very cold. Local police were called in and made a thorough search of the area, which was residential with adjacent public ground. No trace of the child was found. Next day Ulf was brought over; after searching for some time he made his way along a hedge and some distance further on came upon the child lying in a deep ditch, unconscious and suffering from exposure. The dog undoubtedly saved the child's life.

In July 1950 a woman was attacked in a wood and sustained a fractured skull. She was found some time later and taken to hospital. Before losing consciousness she was able to say her assailant wore white gloves. Approximately twenty hours after the attack had taken place Ulf v. Margarethenhof was taken to the spot where the woman was found. He led Harry Darbyshire along one of the many small paths in the wood. Some way along he stopped and after hunting about in some heavy undergrowth he brought out a pair of white gloves, bloodstained. The dog then continued tracking through the wood and out into fields and led his handler across to some wooden bungalows; he stopped beside one which was found to have been broken into. Examination by detectives showed someone had spent the night there, and a search revealed that a gold watch had been stolen. Fingerprints were fo und and a description of the watch was circulated. The following week the watch was offered in pawn in a neighbouring town. The person offering it was arrested; when his fingerprints were taken they were found to be identical with those in the bungalow. The man concerned was convicted. Without the dog there would have been nothing to connect the break-in and subsequent pawn of a stolen watch with the assault in the wood.

Ulf v. Margarethenhof remained in the dog section at Mount-browne until he died in November 1956, aged ten years.

Astor v.d. Morgensonne received his initial training from Alan Osment, one of the three original dog-handlers in the Surrey Constabulary. The dog later passed to other handlers. In December 1950 a man of about eighty was reported missing from Farnham. Astor and his handler joined the search party. The dog found a scent and tracked steadily through undergrowth and down the long steep side of a wood. At the bottom was a stream, where the old man was found lying in the mud suffering from exposure. He was taken home, and recovered.

The Dobermanns bred for police service or used by them are listed in Appendix I. Details are given of the dogs' breeding, their handlers' names and the force with which they worked. Except in the private scrapbooks of the handlers and in the memories of those who worked with the dog sections, few records still remain of cases in which Dobermanns assisted the police in other parts of the country. The following reports have been given by officers of the various forces mentioned, with the permission of the Chief Constable. They are quoted to show the variety of the work done by the dogs.

Mountbrowne Remoh joined the Essex County Constabulary and did some excellent work in the early days of the dog section. A thirteen-year-old girl, asleep in bed, was awakened by a man who committed an indecent assault on her. She screamed and the man leapt from the first-floor window and escaped. About one hour later Remoh arrived with his handler and the dog quickly picked up a track at the foot of a ladder leading to the girl's bedroom. The dog followed the track across the garden and adjoining fields into a nearby army camp, where he crossed the parade ground and continued through the motor transport lines up to a barrack-room hut. The door of the hut was open and the dog went over to a bed where a soldier was sleeping. The soldier was questioned by detectives and later identified by fingerprints found at the scene of the crime. At the quarter sessions later he was convicted of indecent assault.

Mountbrowne Tasco was the first Dobermann used in the Hertfordshire Constabulary and he worked as a police dog for nearly six years. During the first three months of his service he found five missing persons. He was concerned in numerous arrests for crime and was an excellent operational tracking dog.

Mountbrowne Astor was one of the first two dogs used by the Devon Constabulary. This dog proved exceptionally good, particularly for tracking, and he was on active duty until officially retired at the age of twelve years. During this time he was engaged on numerous incidents, brief details of which have been given by a senior officer of the district concerned. In January 1957 Astor assisted in the search for a missing woman on Dartmoor, who was eventually traced and found to be suffering from exposure. Normal attempts to revive her failed and Astor and another dog were used to lie down on each side of her for a period of an hour and a half until she recovered, the body temperature of the dogs being higher than that of a human being.

Astor was concerned in the arrest of ten escaped prisoners, which included six from H.M. Prison on Dartmoor. Of particular interest was the case where one of the escaped prisoners from Dartmoor removed his boots and stockings and walked along the tarmacadam road for a mile and a half to avoid being tracked by police dogs. At the point where the boots and socks were removed Astor indicated that the scent was even stronger and the prisoner was soon located and arrested.

Mountbrowne Onyx went into the dog section of the East Sussex police. Although his handler recommends Alsatians for general work, he says 'I have yet to find any dog equal to the Dobermann for tracking and nosework; his agility also is exceptional.' During his working life Onyx was responsible for twenty-one arrests and for tracing seven missing persons, and in eleven cases was responsible for finding stolen property. One of the latter cases involved jewellery which had been buried under a railway bridge.

The handler particularly remembers one incident when he and Onyx were called to a tearooms where the premises had been broken into and foodstuff stolen. It was two and a half hours before dog and handler arrived. By casting the dog along the verges at each side of the road a track was picked up some 75 to 100 yards from the premises. The dog tracked across country, negotiating thick mud through farmyards and although harrassed by cattle on two occasions he refused to leave the track. He followed it for approximately five miles to a barn, where a tramp was found still sorting out the stolen property.

Mountbrowne Olaf and Mountbrowne Pablo worked with the Cheshire Constabulary. It is said of them: 'Both these dogs gave excellent service as police dogs. . . . It would be true to say that both were good and well up to the standard of Alsatians in use at the time.' Olaf was put to sleep through old age.

One incident concerning Mountbrowne Pablo received considerable Press publicity. One night in January 1963 there was an armed robbery of a taxi driver near to Macclesfield, where Pablo was on patrol with his handler. Soon afterwards they went with other officers to the home of one of two men suspected of being responsible for the robbery. Both these men were known to be of violent disposition. After knocking, the door was opened by a woman who said that her husband and his companion were not in. As the detective-sergeant entered the house a gushing sound was heard and boiling water splashed down from the darkness of the stairway. The handler went forward and sent Pablo up the stairs. There was a crash and a large quantity of a vile-smelling liquid came splashing down on the dog and on the handler's head and face. Pablo yelped with pain and the handler staggered back, blinded by acid and fumes. Two men rushed downstairs and struggled with the police officers, all of whom suffered severe burns from what was later proved to be concentrated nitric acid. The two men were arrested and all the officers were given hospital treatment to their face and eyes.

Pablo was thoroughly examined and treated to counter the effect of the acid but two days later he began to show signs of extensive and severe burns on head, neck and shoulder. After efforts had been made to heal the dog's wounds the Chief Constable decided to have him destroyed on humanitarian grounds. The report ends: 'As a police dog Pablo was very hard and tough and not given to being fondled or petted. He was a very persistent type of dog who never gave up.' The four police officers concerned in this arrest were awarded the Queen's commendation for outstanding police work.

The two Dobermanns first used by the Northumberland County Constabulary were Mountbrowne Amber and Mountbrowne Bruce. Amber went as a young puppy to be brought up by her intended handler, P.C. Jack Hyslop. When he was promoted shortly before her official training was due to begin, P.C. Tom Yeouart took her over. An official photograph of the advanced course at Mountbrowne in March 1957 shows all the dogs were Dobermanns, with Amber at their head. One of her cases was a shopbreaking incident where quantities of cigarettes and chocolates were stolen. Six hours afterwards Amber picked up a scent and tracked for a considerable distance, crossing railway lines and various types of ground. She found small pieces of tobacco on the way and stopped to dig up some packets of cigarettes. She took Tom Yeouart over to one particular tent at a camping-site, he searched it and worked back again, casting the dog free to each side. In two places she found buried quantities of cigarettes and chocolates. In April 1959 Tom Yeouart left the force. Jack Hyslop returned to the dog section as Sergeant in charge and as the handler of Mountbrowne Amber.

In the mid-1950s a Home Office Committee recommended the holding of trials for police dogs, to be organised annually on a national basis and open to handlers representing every city or county force with a dog section. The schedule drawn up at that time has subsequently been changed very little and it covers every aspect of police work in which a dog can be used, the different tests being held over four days. Tests of general obedience and agility are of standard pattern. The criminal work includes an exercise in crowd control as well as the usual tests of courage, chasing, attack and 'stand-off', when after a chase the dog must refrain from biting a stationary figure. Tests of nosework include a long leash-track, a short track on a road or other hard surface, searching a building for a hidden person and searching for articles.

In May 1960, when thirty-three dogs took part, Mountbrowne Amber with her handler Sergeant Hyslop became the first Dobermann ever to win these National Police Dog Trials, finishing fifty marks ahead of the next dog.

In routine police work Mountbrowne Amber worked successfully with both her handlers. Equipment stolen from an explosives store was used for a series of safe-blowing offences in Northumberland, the gang responsible remaining undetected for several months. When three men ran off after being disturbed on locked premises by a patrolling policeman, Amber and Sergeant Hyslop were called in. The dog tracked for several miles through the night across difficult country, ignoring the hazards of cattle, sheep and wandering collie dogs. From a hole in a stone wall she retrieved a lump of gelignite wrapped in a handkerchief and darted back again to bring out a pair of rubber gloves. Using his torch, Jack Hyslop found deep in the hole another pair of gloves, several detonators, wire and a battery. The dog continued to track until daylight when she came out on to a main road, and three men who had been seen to board the early bus at this point were arrested. The equipment found by the dog during the long night's track proved to be identical with that stolen and used in the earlier break-ins.

When the Lancashire Constabulary obtained Mountbrowne Juno from Surrey their dog section also included a tough and somewhat anti-social brown dog, Dober v. Oldenfelde. He had been brought over from Germany and when found to be unsuitable as a family pet he was acquired by the police. To meet the increasing demand for dogs the Lancashire Constabulary kennels became an official breeding and training centre for Alsatians, and Dobermanns were discontinued. In Durham, however, Dobermanns have been used down to the present time. Their kennels too have become an official breeding centre for police dogs, and training courses take place regularly. Many first-class Alsatians have been registered with the Durham Constabulary affix 'Aycliffe'. The Chief Constable, Mr. A. A. Muir, C.B.E., D.L., has always supported the training of Dobermanns for police work and authorised the introduction of new stock from Germany.

After quarantine and a course of training, the imported German dog John v. Waldhorst began regular work. The first time he was on patrol in 1961 his handler was on observation in a car park, following a number of reports of larceny from vehicles and theft of cars. Four youths entered and were overheard discussing which vehicle they should take. One sat on a motor-bike and tried to start it. Another noticed the dog-handler, who challenged them and all ran off. Set loose by his handler, John gave chase, rounded up all four youths and circled them until the handler came up. All were apprehended.

Argus of Aycliffe, when just eighteen months old, was taken by his handler to a builder's yard where a fire during the night had caused extensive damage to timber, stores and lorries. It was thought to be a case of arson. The yard had been the scene of so much activity since the fire was noticed over five hours previously that there seemed little scope for a dog. Noticing scratches on the gate which might have been made by someone climbing over, the handler worked the dog from there. Argus turned away from the gate and tracked steadly into the town, ignoring early shoppers as he went along the pavement of the main street. Although the handler felt it was impossible, the dog seemed to be genuinely following a scent and he tracked right to the door of a house in the residential part of the town. A man who lived there was found to be a former employee at the yard. When taken to the police station, flakes of rust and of paint from the gate and small metal particles from the yard were found on his shoes and clothing. He was charged and taken into custody within seven hours of the fire being started. The police officers in the case were commended for an efficient and well-co-ordinated job. It was established later that the man arrested had taken rags soaked in varnish from his house to start the fire in revenge for his dismissal. The handler believes that the dog tracked on the smell of the varnish from the gate back to the house.

In cities, police dogs can have a useful function. A case has already been quoted where Mountbrowne Pablo assisted in the arrest of two men known to be violent. Dogs had not yet been used by the city police of Newcastle-upon-Tyne when two sergeants of the Durham Constabulary went with their dogs to show how these might be used. The dogs selected were Argus and Arno of Aycliffe. A big warehouse in the city was found to be insecure one night, and required searching for an intruder. On each floor there were great piles of crates, stacked in rows running the whole length of the building. Access to each floor was by a step-ladder without siderails. Argus went in with his handler who sent the dog down and up each row, in turn, to search for anyone who might be concealed between or behind the crates. After each floor was searched Argus went up the ladder to the floor above and worked in the same keen and methodical way. Twenty minutes later the handler reported to the city police that the search was complete and there was no one concealed on the premises. The inspector said that a similarly thorough search using a squad of men normally took half a shift to complete.

One Saturday evening the Durham handlers on patrol with the Newcastle police came upon an inspector, a sergeant and three policemen vainly trying to disperse a noisy crowd emerging from a dance-hall. One handler with his dog went forward and did the job alone, with no delay and no bloodshed. The Newcastle city police now have their own dog patrol.

The Durham Constabulary holds an annual competition for all its police dogs, with tests of obedience, agility, tracking, searching and criminal work. The six dogs with the highest marks then take part in another competition for a trophy and the title of 'Handler of the Year'. In 1960, the total of dogs was eight Dobermanns and eleven Alsatians. In the final, Dobermanns took the first five places with only three-and-a-half marks between them.

Flame of Aycliffe went to the Bedfordshire Constabulary. An official report states that up to her retirement 'Flame had thirty-two arrests to her credit, and this does not include cases where an arrest was made by another officer as a result of work done by the dog'. The report continues that Flame's tracking ability was well-known enough to need no examples and goes on: 'An incident occurred during the early days of the "mod and rocker" era when a large-scale pitched battle took place in the small town of Leighton Buzzard. The inspector in charge called for reinforcements and among them was Flame. This bitch was rather small in stature and did not at first sight have the deterrent value of the more usual Alsatians. Using the dog on a long lead, the handler was able to break up the fight in which some 150 youths were concerned and enabled the other officers present to make a total of seventeen arrests.'

Another Dobermann used in Bedfordshire was Goliath of Dissington. On one occasion Goliath was called late in the evening during a violent rainstorm to a wood where a gamekeeper had disturbed two poachers, who had threatened him with a gun and then made off. By the time the dog arrived five hours had elapsed and that, added to the absolutely impossible conditions, led the handler to believe that the dog would be of no use. However, he cast the dog around in the wood and finding a scent Goliath followed it to a railway embankment, tracking along the embankment and then on the ballast by the railway line. He continued for approximately three miles, during which time he recovered on the track a bag containing game and a twelve-bore shotgun. The track led eventually to the back door of a cottage. When interviewed the occupant of the cottage admitted the offence. The report continues: 'This example goes to show that the Dobermann, a much maligned animal and admittedly less suitable than the German Shepherd dog, can on occasions track in conditions when the average Alsatian would not even start.'

Concerning the three Dobermanns which worked with the Bedfordshire Constabulary (Mountbrowne Yukon, Flame of Aycliffe and Goliath of Dissington) the report adds that 'the Dobermanns, like the Alsatians we use, were patrol dogs working a full eight-hour tour of duty each day, and were in no way regarded as specialists but as valuable members of the Division to which they were attached. The number of occasions when the work of the dog has led to an arrest are many and the type of offences involved varied.'

The Metropolitan Police have used five Dobermanns operationally since 1949. Besides Bowesmoor Hero currently working, previous dogs have been successful; they were called General, Jagga and Duke 9 (a brown). The most famous of the Metropolitan police Dobermanns has been Metpol Fritz, who worked with the same handler throughout eight years of service, from 1954 to 1962, when Fritz died. Metpol Fritz is the only Dobermann to have been awarded the 'Black Knight' Trophy, donated by Lady

Munnings, which is presented each year to the best all-round Metropolitan police dog. Fritz won the trophy in 1959.

In May 1958, as a result of tracking a 'look-out man' to a sub-urban railway station at about midnight, two men found there breaking open a safe were surprised by Metpol Fritz and his handler. The men leapt out of the window to the pavement 20 feet below. Dog and handler followed and the officer fell on one man, who was arrested. Fritz was severely winded and his handler broke his ankle. While on sick leave the officer made persistent enquiries and eventually arrested the second man. The officer and his dog were commended.

When an emergency arises and the local police forces have no dogs of their own (a rare occurrence today), civilian dogs are sometimes called in to help. When a child or an old person has been reported missing obviously the larger the search-party the better, and in the past members of many training clubs have come with their dogs to lend assistance. An unusual call was made to Dobermann Club member Michael Garrod, who with his bitch Dena of Illustria joined in the search for a wolf which had escaped from Whipsnade Zoo.

Before there were any police dogs in Scotland north of the Tay two civilian Dobermanns were on call for emergencies, and besides taking part in several searches for missing persons they were used in the following-up of long-term prisoners who had escaped. My dog Vyking Drum Major was called out for the first time one dark and windy evening after a prisoner had broken away from a working party at dusk. The dog had no previous experience of working at night but he tracked across fields and ploughed land, negotiating walls, ditches and wire fences, with the escort of police and prison officers sometimes treading on the tracking-line in their enthusiasm. After some three miles the track was lost in churned-up ground near a farmhouse. From a telephone call to HQ the search-party learned that the prisoner had just been re-captured as he reached a main road less than half a mile ahead. During the track, whenever the dog had changed direction a police officer with the group left to report their position by tele-phone, and police cars had thus been ready on the road when their customer arrived.

One cold dry February morning in 1958 a well-known safe-breaker went 'over the wall' of one of Scotland's big prisons and was noticed walking down the main road by a prison officer going on duty. When challenged the prisoner ran off. The alarm was given and, when Lorelei of Tavey and I were brought two hours later to help in the search, the road near the prison was crowded with cars and spectators. A jacket belonging to the prisoner was brought for the dog to identify his scent, and when the tracking-harness was put on she worked slowly along each side of the road. She then tracked steadily and with intense concentration from the grass verge along the road and down a gravel lane towards the local school. Police officers behind called to me to stop the dog as the school building had already been searched. The rest of the day was spent in unsuccessful searches elsewhere. Next morning the prisoner was recaptured a short distance away. He told the police that he had gone up the fire escape and had spent all the previous day on the roof of the school. It would appear the dog had correctly picked out and followed his scent among the lighter footsteps of the children going later to school.

In November 1954 the Association of Chief Constables formed a Working Party on Police Dogs. One of their many important recommendations was the setting up of the Standing Advisory Committee on Police Dogs under the chairmanship of H.M. Inspector of Constabulary. This committee set up the regional and National Police Dog Trials, the first of which were held in July 1958.

A recommendation of the Working Party made in June 1957 was that: 'The Alsatian is considered to be the most suitable breed for police work, although there is no reason why other breeds which are found to be suitable for police work should not be used.' This view was later endorsed by the Standing Advisory Committee and experience since has shown no reason for revision.

Opinions for and against the Dobermann are held equally strongly by those who love and those who heartily dislike the breed, and in any argument on the subject as much prejudice is shown by one side as by the other. However much enthusiastic supporters would like to see the Dobermann used more often by the police there are a number of reasons why the Alsatian is preferred. In the eyes of the general public the Alsatian is more impressive, powerful and alert, with pricked ears and an appearance that enforces respect and often fear. On patrol the Alsatian is ever-watchful and looks the part whatever he is doing. A Dobermann easily gets bored and needs some movement or noise or an incident to arouse its interest, when it becomes instantly equally effective.

As it was the late Sir Joseph Simpson who started Dobermanns working for the police it is perhaps appropriate to end by quoting from an article he wrote for a feature on the breed in *Dog World* of May 28, 1954. Permission to quote from his article on 'Dobermann Pinschers as Police Dogs' was given by his widow, the late Lady Simpson, and by the proprietors of *Dog World*.

'Our aims [i.e. at Mountbrowne] have been to produce the attributes of a good working dog, concentrating on nose, temperament, strength, speed and stamina. . . . The strong point about a Dobermann is that he is a first-class tracker, indeed second to none in this department. Its advantages in tracking are an extremely sensitive nose, with stamina and speed and the ability to continue through extreme heat and over parched ground. . . . When a dog is highly trained it will keep its nose close to the ground and hardly raise it from the track. It then appears to be tracking at a modest walk, but a timed speed of any given distance will surprise those who are watching. The dog has been proved to be resolute and to compare favourably with the finest examples of other breeds in criminal and manwork. The greenest novice must admit that a Dobermann's reactions are the quickest that can be witnessed.

'As the breed has its strong points so too it must admit to weaknesses. The short coat which stands it in such good stead in hot weather is a handicap in cold. The Dobermann must be housed more carefully in winter than other breeds. While he will track under the coldest and most penetrating conditions without apparent ill-effect, the dog displays great discomfort if required to remain still in the open with his handler, as when keeping observation through long hours of winter weather. There is a tendency to moodiness and wilfulness in the Dobermann and unless sympathetically handled he can easily be spoilt. He matures later than most breeds which must be taken into account in training and handling.

'The Dobermann when working is undoubtedly spectacular and to the uninitiated it has a great appeal. It is hard to make people asking for advice on the subject realise, until they learn by bitter experience, that the Dobermann is not really the dog for a novice handler, unless that handler is under continuous expert supervision by someone experienced in the intricacies of the breed.'

KENNEL CLUB REGISTRATION TOTALS

1948	—	Nil	1964 — 875	
1949	—	Nil	1965 — 789	
1950	—	Nil	1966 — 1017	
1951	—	94	1967 — 1119	
1952	—	112	1968 — 1528	
1953	—	138	1969 — 1553	
1954	—	135	1970 — 1645	
1955	—	205	1971 — 1566	
1956	—	189	1972 — 1594	
1957	—	241	1973 — 1891	
1958	—	236	1974 — 2029	
1959	—	358	1975 — 2265	
1960	—	385	1976 — 920*	
1961	—	510	1977 — 594	
1962	—	608	1978 — 1336	
1963	—	567	1979 (Jan–May) 1537	

Note: From 1948 to 1950 all puppies were registered under 'Any other variety'.

*The new system of registration adopted in 1976, mainly to record dogs intended for competition or export, proved complicated and created many difficulties and delays. This accounts for what may seem a drop in the registration totals for 1976 and 1977, when in fact many more Dobermanns were born during these years than previously. In February 1978 another change was made in the system of recording, and gradually the backlog of registrations which had built up since 1976 is being reduced.

BREED CLUBS

THE DOBERMANN CLUB
Secretary
Mrs. E. C. Eales
Oak House, Widford, Nr. Ware, Herts

MIDLAND DOBERMANN CLUB
Secretary
Mrs. Joyce Window
Heather Dene Boarding Kennels,
Matlock Moor, Matlock, Derbyshire, DE4 5PX

NORTH OF ENGLAND DOBERMANN CLUB
Secretary
Mr. David Brown
48 Park Avenue, Sale, Cheshire, M33 1HE

SCOTTISH DOBERMANN CLUB
Secretary
Mr. Alan Leggett
49 King Street, Stonehouse, Strathclyde, ML9 3EQ

WELSH DOBERMANN CLUB
Secretary
Mrs. V. Mulholland
Forge Cottage, Cwmavon, nr. Port Talbot,
West Glamorgan

AMERICAN KENNEL CLUB STANDARD OF THE DOBERMANN PINSCHER

(Adopted by the Doberman Pinscher Club of America and approved by the Board of Directors of the American Kennel Club, October, 1969).

GENERAL CONFORMATION AND APPEARANCE

The appearance is that of a dog of medium size, with a body that is square; the height, measured vertically from the ground to the highest point of the withers, equalling the length measured horizontally from the forechest to the rear projection of the upper thigh. *Height* at the withers—*Dogs* 26 to 28 inches, ideal about $27\frac{1}{2}$ inches; *Bitches* 24 to 26 inches, ideal about $25\frac{1}{2}$ inches. Length of head, neck and legs in proportion to length and depth of body. Compactly built, muscular and powerful, for great endurance and speed. Elegant in appearance, of proud carriage, reflecting great nobility and temperament. Energetic, watchful, determined, alert, fearless, loyal and obedient.

The judge shall dismiss from the ring any shy or vicious Doberman.

Shyness—A dog shall be judged fundamentally shy if, refusing to stand for examination, it shrinks away from the judge; if it fears an approach from the rear; if it shies at sudden and unusual noises to a marked degree.

Viciousness—A dog that attacks or attempts to attack either the judge or its handler, is definitely vicious. An aggressive or belligerent attitude towards other dogs shall not be deemed viciousness.

HEAD

Long and dry, resembling a blunt wedge in both frontal and profile views. When seen from the front, the head widens gradually toward the base of the ears in a practically unbroken line. Top of skull flat, turning with slight stop to bridge of muzzle, with muzzle line extending parallel to top line of skull. Cheeks flat and muscular. Lips lying close to jaws. Jaws full and powerful, well filled under the eyes.

Eyes—Almond shaped, moderately deep set, with vigorous, energetic expression. Iris, of uniform color, ranging from medium to darkest brown in black dogs; in reds, blues, and fawns the color of the iris blends with that of the markings, the darkest shade being preferable in every case.

Teeth—Strongly developed and white. Lower incisors upright and touching inside of upper incisors—a true scissors bite. *42 correctly placed teeth*, 22 in the lower, 20 in the upper jaw. Distemper teeth shall not be penalized.

Disqualifying Faults—Overshot more than $\frac{3}{16}$ of an inch. Undershot more than $\frac{1}{8}$ of an inch. Four or more missing teeth.

Ears—Normally cropped and carried erect. The upper attachment of the ear, when held erect, is on a level with the top of the skull.

NECK

Proudly carried, well muscled and dry. Well arched, with nape of neck widening gradually toward body. Length of neck proportioned to body and head.

BODY

Back short, firm, of sufficient width, and muscular at the lions, extending in a straight line from withers to the *slightly* rounded croup.

Withers—pronounced and forming the highest point of the body. *Brisket* reaching deep to the elbow. *Chest* broad with forechest well defined. *Ribs* well sprung from the spine, but flattened in lower end to permit elbow clearance. *Belly* well tucked up, extending in a curved line from the brisket. *Lions* wide and muscled. *Hips* broad and in proportion to body, breadth of hips being approximately equal to breadth of body at rib cage and shoulders. *Tail* docked at approximately second joint, appears to be a continuation of the spine, and is carried only slightly above the horizontal when the dog is alert.

FOREQUARTERS

Shoulder Blade sloping forward and downward at a 45 degree angle to the ground meets the upper arm at an angle of 90 degrees. Length of shoulder blade and upper arm are equal. Height from elbow to withers approximately equals height from ground to elbow. *Legs,* seen from front and side, perfectly straight and parallel to each other from elbow to pastern: muscled and sinewy, with heavy bone. In normal pose and when gaiting, the elbows lie close to the brisket. *Pasterns* firm and almost perpendicular to the ground. *Feet* well arched, compact, and catlike, turning neither in nor out. Dewclaws may be removed.

HINDQUARTERS

The angulation of the hindquarters balances that of the forequarters. *Hip Bone* falls away from spinal column at an angle of about 30 degrees, producing a slightly rounded, well-filled-out croup. *Upper Shanks,* at right angles to the hip bones, are long, wide, and well muscled on both sides of thigh, with clearly defined stifles. Upper and lower shanks are of equal length. While the dog is at rest, hock to heel is perpendicular to the ground. Viewed from the rear, the legs are straight, parallel to each other, and wide enough apart to fit in with a properly built body. *Cat Feet,* as on front legs, turning neither in nor out. Dewclaws, if any, are generally removed.

GAIT

Free, balanced, and vigorous, with good reach in the forequarters and good driving power in the hindquarters. When trotting, there is strong rear-action drive. Each rear leg moves in line with the foreleg on the same side. Rear and front legs are thrown neither in nor out. Back remains strong and firm. When moving at a fast trot, a properly built dog will singletrack.

COAT, COLOR, MARKINGS

Coat, smooth-haired, short, hard, thick and close lying. Invisible gray undercoat on neck permissible.
Allowed Colors—Black, red, blue, and fawn (Isabella). *Markings*—Rust, sharply defined, appearing above each eye and on muzzle,

throat and forechest, on all legs and feet, and below tail. *Nose* solid black on black dogs, dark brown on red ones, dark gray on blue ones, dark tan on fawns. White patch on chest, not exceeding $\frac{1}{2}$ square inch, permissible.

FAULTS—THE FOREGOING DESCRIPTION IS THAT OF THE IDEAL DOBERMAN PINSCHER. ANY DEVIATION FROM THE ABOVE DESCRIBED DOG MUST BE PENALIZED TO THE EXTENT OF THE DEVIATION.

DISQUALIFICATIONS

OVERSHOT MORE THAN $\frac{3}{16}$ OF AN INCH; UNDERSHOT MORE THAN $\frac{1}{8}$ OF AN INCH. FOUR OR MORE MISSING TEETH.

The following scale of points is to be used only as a guide to breeders and to apprentice judges. It is *not* to be employed in the ring and is not to considered as part of the approved Standard.

SCALE OF POINTS

1 GENERAL CONFORMATION AND APPEARANCE
Proportions 8
Bone ⎫
Substance ⎬ 8
Temperament ⎫
Expression ⎬ 8
Nobility ⎭
Condition 5
— 29

2 HEAD
Shape 6
Teeth 5
Eyes 3
Ears 1
— 15

3 NECK   3
                                                        —   3

4 BODY
  Backline   ⎫
  Withers   ⎬   8
  Loins   ⎪
  Tail Placement ⎭
  Chest   ⎫
  Brisket   ⎬   8
  Rib Spring   ⎪
  Tuck-up   ⎭
  Shape and proportions   4
                                                        —   20

5 FOREQUARTERS
  Shoulders   ⎫
  Upper arms   ⎬   5
  Legs   ⎪
  Pasterns   ⎭
  Angulation   4
  Paws   2
                                                        —   11

6 HINDQUARTERS
  Upper thigh   ⎫
  Stifle   ⎬   5
  Hocks   ⎭
  Angulation   4
  Paws   2
                                                        —   11

7 GAIT   6
                                                        —   6

8 COAT
  Colour   ⎫   5
  Markings   ⎭   —   5
  Total   100   100

SOME INFLUENTIAL SIRES AND DAMS

Ch. & Ob. Ch. Jupiter of Tavey

- Bruno of Tavey
  - Benno v.d. Schwedenhecke
  - Pia v.d. Dobberhof
- Prinses Anja v't Scheepjeskerk
  - Graaf Dagobert v. Neerlands Stam
  - Alindia v't Scheepjeskerk

Prinses Anja v't Scheepjeskerk

- Graaf Dagobert v. Neerlands Stam
  - Waldo v.d. Wachtparade
  - Roeanka v.d. Rhederveld
- Alindia v't Scheepjeskerk
  - Bucko v.d. Heerhof
  - Andranette v. Rio de la Plata

Bruno of Tavey

- Benno v.d. Schwedenhecke
  - Faust v.d. Nievelsburg
  - Kitty v. Friedwald
- Pia v.d. Dobberhof
  - Brando v. Berggreef
  - Alie v.d. Heerhof

Ch. Tavey's Stormy Achievement

- **Tasso v.d. Eversburg of Tavey**
  - Alex v. Kleinwaldheim
    - Ajax v. Simbach
    - Carola v. Sudharz
  - Christel v. Brunoberg
    - Frido v. Rauhfelsen
    - Unruh v. Sandberg
- **Cartergate Alpha of Tavey**
  - Derb v. Brunoberg
    - Axel v.d. Germania
    - Unruh v. Sandberg
  - Beka v. Brunoberg
    - Frido v. Rauhfelsen
    - Unruh v. Sandberg
- **Am.Ch. Rancho Dobe's Storm**
  - Am.Ch. Rancho Dobe's Primo
    - Am.Ch. Alcor v. Millsdod
    - Am.Ch. Rancho Dobe's Kashmir
  - Am.Ch. Maedel v. Randahof
    - Mr. Butch v. Rittenhouse
    - Am.Ch. Indra v. Lindehof
- **Am.Ch. Rustic Adagio**
  - Am.Ch. Rancho Dobe's Storm
    - Am.Ch. Rancho Dobe's Primo
    - Am.Ch. Maedel v. Randahof
  - Am.Ch. Rustic Adagio
    - Am. & Int.Ch. Kilburn Ideal
    - Rustic Radiance

Ch. Tavey's Stormy Abundance

- Am.Ch. Rancho Dobe's Storm
  - Am.Ch. Rancho Dobe's Primo
  - Am.Ch. Maedel v. Randahof
- Am.Ch. Rustic Adagio
  - Am. & Int.Ch. Kilburn Ideal
  - Rustic Radiance

Am.Ch. Steb's Top Skipper

- Am.Ch. Dortmund Delly's Colonel Jet
  - Am.Ch. Delegate v.d. Elbe
  - Tuzieher Lady Ambercrest
- Damasyn the Easter Bonnet
  - Am.Ch. Rancho Dobe's Storm
  - Damasyn Sikhandi

Ch. Acclamation of Tavey

- Am.Ch. Steb's Top Skipper
  - Am.Ch. Dortmund Delly's Colonel Jet
  - Damasyn the Easter Bonnet
- Orebaugh's Raven of Tavey
  - Am.Ch. Rancho Dobe's Primo
  - Am.Ch. Orebaugh's Gentian

Am.Ch. Rustic Adagio of Tavey

- Am. & Int.Ch. Kilburn Ideal
  - Am.Ch. Dow's Dusty v. Keinlesberg
  - Am.Ch. Dow's Illena of Marienland
- Rustic Radiance
  - Am.Ch. Gunther v. Westphalia
  - Kilburn Jiffy

Tavey's Stormy Governess
- Ch. Tavey's Stormy Achievement
  - Am.Ch. Rancho Dobe's Storm
  - Am.Ch. Rustic Adagio
- Tamara of Tavey
  - Tasso v.d. Eversburg of Tavey
  - Prinses Anja v't Scheepjeskerk

Ch. Iceberg of Tavey
- Ch. Acclamation of Tavey
  - Am. Ch. Steb's Top Skipper
  - Orebaugh's Raven of Tavey
- Juno of Cartergate
  - Ch. Claus of Cartergate
  - Ch. Helena of Cartergate

Ch. Triogen Traffic Cop
- Ch. Acclamation of Tavey
  - Am.Ch. Steb's Top Skipper
  - Orebaugh's Raven of Tavey
- Triogen Teenage Sensation
  - Triogen Top Lad
  - Triogen Tullaherin

Phileen's Duty Free of Tavey
- Am.Ch. Tarrado's Corry
  - Am.Ch. Felix v. Ahrtal
  - Am.Ch. Highbriar Jasmine
- Kay Hill's Outrigger
  - Am.Ch. Dolph v. Tannenwald
  - Kay Hill's Kat a Maran

Tavey's Satellite
- Am.Ch. Kay Hill's Dealers Choice
  - Am.Ch. Dolph v. Tannenwald
  - Kay Hill's Kat a Maran
- Arawak Perfecta
  - Am.Ch. Dolph v. Tannenwald
  - Arawak Hi-A-Leah C.D.

Vanessa's Little Dictator of Tavey
- Am.Ch. Checkmate Chessman
  - Am.Ch. Alemaps Checkmate
  - Am.Ch. Wallmars Baroness
- Am. Ch. Valheim's Vanessa
  - Am.Ch. Alemaps Checkmate
  - Am.Ch. Campeons Tenta Dora

Nieta of Tavey
- Vanessa's Little Dictator of Tavey
  - Am.Ch. Checkmate Chessman
  - Am.Ch. Valheim's Vanessa
- Tavey's Distinctive Daneen
  - Am.Ch. Marks Tey Hanover
  - Am.Ch. Dodie of Marks Tey C.D.

BREED CHAMPIONS TO DECEMBER 1979

Name	Sex	Birth	Sire	Dam	Owner	Breeder
Sheumac Storm	M	6-7-51	Wolfox Birling Rogue	Belle of Upend	G. A. Tunnicliffe	Mrs. E. A. Sandland
Wolfox Birling Rogue	M	23-2-49	Birling Bruno v. Ehrgarten	Birling Britta v.d. Heerhof	Mrs. B. Douglas-Redding	L. Hamilton-Renwick
Empress of Tavey	F	28-8-50	Bruno of Tavey	Prinses Anja v't Scheepjeskerk	Miss J. Skinner	Mrs. J. Curnow
Elegant of Tavey	F	28-8-50	Bruno of Tavey	Prinses Anja v't Scheepjeskerk	Mrs. J. Curnow	Owner
Alli of Girton	M	14-8-51	Djonja of Upend	Bernadette of Upend	H. Greenhalgh	K. E. Kitteridge
Bridget of Upend	F	21-3-50	Birling Roimond	Freida v. Casa Mia of Upend	Mrs. J. Richardson	Mrs. B. Butler
Lyric of Tavey	F	28-9-52	Tasso v.d. Eversburg of Tavey	Prinses Anja v't Scheepjeskerk	Mrs. J. Curnow	Owner
Lustre of Tavey	M	28-9-52	Tasso v.d. Eversburg of Tavey	Prinses Anja v't Scheepjeskerk	Mrs. J. Curnow	Owner
Claus of Cartergate	M	30-5-52	Birling Roimond	Cartergate Alpha of Tavey	L. R. Thorne-Dunn	Miss E. M. Would
Caprice of Cartergate	F	30-5-52	Birling Roimond	Cartergate Alpha of Tavey	J. T. Foers	Miss E. M. Would

Name	Sex	Date	Sire	Dam		
Francesca of Fulton	F	13-5-51	Wolfox Birling Rogue	Birling Rachel	Mrs. J. Currie	C. L. Hamilton-Renwick
Juno of Tavey	F	22-3-52	Bruno of Tavey	Prinses Anja v't Scheepjeskerk	L. R. Thorne-Dunn	Mrs. J. Curnow
Jupiter of Tavey	M	22-3-52	Bruno of Tavey	Prinses Anja v't Scheepjeskerk	Mrs. J. Curnow	Owner
Precept of Tavey	M	3-9-53	Tasso v.d. Eversburg of Tavey	Elegant of Tavey	Mrs. E. M. Cathcart	Mrs. J. Curnow
Mahadeo Brown Berrie	F	19-1-54	Jupiter of Tavey	Empress of Tavey	Miss J. Skinner	Mr. & Mrs. A. Thompson
Adges Going Places	F	2-7-53	Tasso v.d. Eversburg of Tavey	Helga v. Kleinwaldheim	Misses J. Skinner & M. Menzies	Miss A. Langsdon
Rhythm of Tavey	F	28-6-54	Bruno of Tavey	Gloss of Tavey	Mrs. J. Curnow	Owner
Daybreak of Cartergate	M	15-3-54	Tasso v.d. Eversburg of Tavey	Cartergate Alpha of Tavey	S. J. Taylor	Miss E. M. Would
Day of Cartergate	M	15-3-54	Tasso v.d. Eversburg of Tavey	Cartergate Alpha of Tavey	Miss E. M. Would	Owner
Reichert Judy	F	18-5-52	Bill v. Blauen Blut	Birling Rachel	Sgt. Darbyshire & Mrs. M. Porterfield	Mrs. J. McHardy
Xel of Tavey	F	15-6-55	Adel of Tavey	Lacrosse Up and Doing	Mrs. M. Bastable	Mrs. J. Curnow
Challenger of Sonhende	M	24-7-54	Claus of Cartergate	Juno of Tavey	R. H. Jackson	L. R. Thorne-Dunn
Ace of Tavey	M	25-4-50	Bruno of Tavey	Beka v. Brunoberg	Mrs. V. Simons	Mrs. J. Curnow
Bowesmoor Mona	F	25-5-57	Treu v. Steinfurthohe	Reichert Judy	G. Thompson	Mrs. M. Porterfield
Carrickgreen Walda Nagasta	F	20-4-57	Alex v. Rodenaer	Barnelms Bess	P. Clark	M. Migliorini

Name	Sex	Birth	Sire	Dam	Owner	Breeder
Satin of Tavey	F	21-8-54	Bruno of Tavey	Elegant of Tavey	Mrs. D. Horton	Mrs. J. Curnow
Tavey's Stormy Abundance	M	7-5-56	Rancho Dobe's Storm	Rustic Adagio	Mrs. J. Curnow	Owner
Tavey's Stormy Adagio	F	7-5-56	Rancho Dobe's Storm	Rustic Adagio	Mrs. J. Curnow	Owner
Tavey's Stormy Acacia	M	7-5-56	Rancho Dobe's Storm	Rustic Adagio	Mrs. J. Curnow	Owner
Tavey's Stormy Daughter	F	20-11-57	Tavey's Stormy Achievement	Tamara of Tavey	E. Protheroe	Mrs. J. Curnow
Baba Black Pepper	F	7-1-57	Bruno of Tavey	Pia v.d. Dobberhof	Mrs. Ince	Mrs. H. Hewitson
Caliph of Trevellis	M	5-4-58	Tavey's Stormy Abundance	Satin of Tavey	E. Plumb	Mrs. D. Horton
Talaureen Hurricane	M	25-7-56	Jupiter of Tavey	Quicksilver of Tavey	Mrs. E. Barnacle	Miss E. Tatler
Tavey's Stormy Achievement	M	7-5-54	Rancho Dobe's Storm	Rustic Adagio	Mrs. J. Curnow	Owner
Venture of Vreda	F	17-6-58	Tavey's Stormy Abundance	Ardent of Trevellis	N. Thatcher	Mrs. A. Thomas
Auldrigg Corsair	M	15-8-58	Tavey's Stormy Achievement	Fascination of Sonhende	W. Gallaher	A. Auld
Acclamation of Tavey	M	2-7-59	Steb's Top Skipper	Orebaugh's Raven of Tavey	Mrs. J. Curnow	Owner
Cordelia of Trevellis	F	5-7-58	Tavey's Stormy Abundance	Satin of Tavey	Mr. C. Starns	Mrs. D. Horton
Helena of Cartergate	F	27-2-57	Precept of Tavey	Lola of Cartergate	Miss E. M. Would	Owner

Name	Sex	Date	Sire	Dam		Owner
Tumlow Storm Caesar	M	27-7-59	Tavey's Stormy Achievement	Baba Black Pepper	Mrs. Platt	Miss E. Hoxey
Tavey's Stormy Leprechaun	F	28-10-59	Tavey's Stormy Abundance	Utopia of Tavey	E. Protheroe	M. Theobald
Tumlow Fantasy	F	14-6-60	Acclamation of Tavey	Tavey's Stormy Governess	Miss E. Hoxey	Mrs. J. Curnow and Miss E. Hoxey
Tavey's Stormy Objective	M	29-6-60	Tavey's Stormy Achievement	Orebaugh's Raven of Tavey	Mrs. J. Curnow	Owner
Annastock Lance	M	26-7-62	Tavey's Stormy Achievement	Annastock Amberlili of Catharden	Mrs. J. Parkes	Owner
Caliph of Barrimilne	M	30-4-48	Tavey's Stormy Achievement	Xel of Tavey	Mr. Fagot	Mrs. M. Bastable
Jove of Cartergate	M	6-8-59	Claus of Cartergate	Helena of Cartergate	Miss E. M. Would	Owner
Tavey's Stormy Wrath	F	25-5-61	Acclamation of Tavey	Tavey's Stormy Governess	Mrs. J. Curnow	Mrs. J. Curnow and Miss E. Hoxey
Tavey's Stormy Wonder	M	25-5-61	Acclamation of Tavey	Tavey's Stormy Governess	Mrs. J. Curnow	Mrs. J. Curnow and Miss E. Hoxey
Tavey's Stormy Nugget	M	14-4-60	Acclamation of Tavey	Tavey's Stormy Governess	F. Williams	Mrs. J. Curnow and Miss E. Hoxey
Adoration of Dumbrill	F	25-4-60	Tavey's Stormy Abundance	Utopia of Tavey	M. Theobald	Owner
Dolina Naiad	F	16-2-61	Acclamation of Tavey	Gypsy of Sonhende	Mrs. F. Auld	Mrs. S. Atkinson
Tavey's Stormy Master	M	25-4-60	Tavey's Stormy Abundance	Utopia of Tavey	H. Inskip	M. Theobald

Name	Sex	Birth	Sire	Dam	Owner	Breeder
Tumlow Impeccable	M	25-5-61	Acclamation of Tavey	Tavey's Stormy Governess	Miss E. Hoxey	Miss E. Hoxey and Mrs. J. Curnow
Tumlow Whinlands Flurry	F	16-1-62	Acclamation of Tavey	Tumlow Storm Away	Miss E. Hoxey	Mrs. E. Hewan
Wyndenhelm's AWOL	F	25-7-60	Caliph of Trevellis	Bowesmoor Mona	G. Thompson	Owner
Ampherlaw Sir Galahad	M	25-3-62	Auldrigg Corsair	Ampherlaw Gretel	H. Hogg	Mrs. G. Brandon
Carrickgreen Confederate	M	10-2-59	Tavey's Stormy Abundance	Carrickgreen Walda Nagasta	Mrs. C. McNee	P. Clark
Dolina Nereid	F	16-1-61	Acclamation of Tavey	Gypsy of Sonhende	Mrs. S. Atkinson	Owner
Edencourt's Avenger	M	27-4-62	Acclamation of Tavey	Tavey's Stormy Daughter	Mrs. A. Hewitt	E. Protheroe
Hans of Tickwillow	M	24-4-61	Tavey's Stormy Abundance	Trudi of Ely	W. A. Hopkin	Owner
Iceberg of Tavey	M	16-8-63	Acclamation of Tavey	Juno of Cartergate	Mrs. J. Curnow	Mrs. J. Curnow and Miss E. Would
Achteloch Heidi	F	21-3-63	Acclamation of Tavey	Tumlow Storm Charmer	Mr. McLeod	Mrs. B. Pope
Gurnard Gemma	F	1-11-63	Acclamation of Tavey	Gurnard Hedda	Mr. Barnard & Mrs. Billingham	Barnard/Billingham
Tavey's Stormy Willow	F	25-5-61	Acclamation of Tavey	Tavey's Stormy Governess	C. Starns	Mrs. J. Curnow and Miss E. Hoxey
Tumlow Katrina	F	16-6-63	Tavey's Stormy Achievement	Tumlow Fantasy	Miss E. Pudney	Miss E. Hoxey

Name	Sex	Date	Sire	Dam	Breeder	Owner
Cadereyta of Roanoke	F	30-5-64	Tumlow Impeccable	Heide of Tickwillow	Mrs. D. Richardson	D. Hodson
Crontham King	M	12-10-63	Annastock Lance	Tavey's Stormy Queen	G. Gilfillam	R. Whittle
Empress of Bute	F	23-2-64	Dirksby's Arcadian of Tavey	Maid of Bute	Miss P. Wilson	Owner
Opinion of Tavey	F	19-10-64	Acclamation of Tavey	Juno of Cartergate	Mrs. J. Ryan	Mrs. J. Curnow
Oberan of Tavey	M	19-10-64	Acclamation of Tavey	Juno of Cartergate	M. Gover	Mrs. J. Curnow
Triogen Traffic Cop	M	8-2-63	Acclamation of Tavey	Triogen Teenage Sensation	A. Hogg	Owner
Triogen Tuppenny Feast	F	29-5-64	Acclamation of Tavey	Triogen Teenage Wonder	Mrs. D. Richardson	A. Hogg
Triogen Tuppenny Treat	F	29-5-64	Acclamation of Tavey	Triogen Teenage Wonder	Mrs. J. Scheja	A. Hogg
Clanguard Comanche	M	9-8-64	Carrickgreen Confederate	Fricka of Codmore	Mrs. H. Morgan	M. J. Beattie
Carlagon Ravishing	F	23-7-65	Acclamation of Tavey	Triogen Tarragon	L. Lock	Owner
Heidiland Trouble Spot	M	18-4-65	Tavey's Stormy Achievement	Triogen Traffic Trouble	R. Selbourne	Miss A. Chaffey
Kassel of Royaltain	F	4-4-64	Acclamation of Tavey	Barrimiline Helga	Miss P. Quinn	Owner
Tramerfield's Dubonny Princess	F	25-11-65	Tumlow Storm Caesar	Capri of Tramerfield	J. Hall	Owner
Delmordene Buccaneer	M	21-7-65	Crontham King	Achenburg Heidi	J. Bramley	Owner
Bronvorny's Explorer	M	27-4-64	Tavey's Stormy Achievement	Triogen Tuff Talk	Mrs. B. Barry	Mrs. Harper

Name	Sex	Birth	Sire	Dam	Owner	Breeder
Nayrilla Athene	F	26-4-67	Vanessa's Little Dictator	Opinion of Tavey	Mrs. P. Mitchell	Mrs. J. Ryan
Skybank Tango	F	11-9-66	Edencourts Banker	Skyline Tuta	I. Williams	P. Tompkyns
Triogen Tornado	M	20-3-67	Triogen Traffic Cop	Triogen Treble Chance	A. Hogg	Owner & Mrs. Kelly
Wismar of Royaltain	F	24-1-66	Tumlow Impeccable	Barrimilne Helga	Mrs. S. Chambers	Miss P. Quinn
Clanguard Cadet	M	30-8-65	Carrickgreen Confederate	Fricka of Codmore	A. Montgomery	Mr. W. Blantyre
Baroness of Tavey	F	4-11-66	Vanessa's Little Dictator	Westwinds Quint-essence of Tavey	Mrs. V. Killip	Mrs. J. Curnow
Dizzy Debutante	F	5-7-65	Iceberg of Tavey	Tavey's Stormy Kamella	Mrs. D. Hart	Mrs. Gillespie
Nagold of Royaltain	B	25-11-67	Tumlow Impeccable	Barrimilne Helga	Mrs. D. Yule	Miss P. Quinn
Nayrilla Adonis	M	22-4-67	Vanessa's Little Dictator	Opinion of Tavey	Mrs. D. Neale	Mrs. J. Ryan
Royaltain's Babette of Tavey	F	4-11-66	Vanessa's Little Dictator	Westwinds Quint-essence of Tavey	P. Quinn & P. Gledhill	Mrs. J. Curnow
Kingroy Karla Kay	F	8-3-68	Stormy Baron	Devi's Hurricane	Witham & O'Connor	G. White
Rajada Juliet	F	30-5-64	Tumlow Impeccable	Heidi of Tickwillow	R. Hodge	D. Hodson
Rioghal Raquel	F	16-4-67	Cubist of Tavey	Clanguard Cantata	L. Galbraith	M. Grierson

178

Name	Sex	Date	Sire	Dam	Breeder	Owner
Tavey's Stormy Medallion	M	26-3-64	Tavey's Stormy Achievement	Tavey's Stormy Willow	Mrs. D. Parker	Mrs. C. Starns
Royaltain's Reluctant Hero's	M	9-6-68	Heidiland Trouble Spot	Kassel of Royaltain	H. Astley	Miss P. Quinn
Achim Zeitgeist	M	19-10-66	Tavey's Stormy Nugget	Tavey's Stormy Pride	Mrs. G. Bradshaw	Mrs. Parkes and Mr. Bradshaw
Hensel Midnight Max	M	7-11-67	Tavey's Stormy Medallion	Barrimilne Black Diamond	Miss C. Parker	Mr. & Mrs. G. Henson
Roanoke Bobadilla	F	9-5-68	Roanoke Nayrilla Apollo	Cadereyta of Roanoke	J. & Mrs. D. Richardson	Owners
Achenburg Delilah	F	18-6-68	Achim Zeitgeist	Katina of Trevellis	Mrs. M. Woodward	Owner
Tumlow Bonanza	F	13-5-69	Tumlow Impeccable	Tumlow Odette	Mr. & Mrs. R. Harris	Mr. O. Powell
Tumlow Whiplash	M	18-6-68	Tumlow Peter Royal	Tumlow the Witch	Mr. & Mrs. R. Harris	A. Barnard
Nordosten Kantata	F	20-3-70	Clanguard Cadet	Xantippe of Sonhende	Mrs. J. Crawshaw	Owner
Auldrigg Pinza	M	3-6-70	Tumlow Impeccable	Tumlow Odette	Mrs. A. Wilson	Mrs. F. Auld
Ecstasy of Tramerfield	F	12-10-68	Edencourts Avenger	Tramerfield Du-Bonny Princess	Mrs. R. Anderson	J. Hall
Linhoff Pearl Diver	F	25-10-69	Wilm von Forell	Linhoff Triogen Tessa	K. Frankland	Owner
Tumlow Aerolite	F	28-2-69	Edencourts Banker	Tavey's Stormy Pepita	Mrs. N. Hewan	Mr. & Mrs. R. Harris
Tumlow Carousel	F	15-6-69	Tumlow Impeccable	Tumlow Blue Charm	Mrs. R. McAleese	Mr. & Mrs. R. Harris
Tumlow Satan	M	2-3-68	Tumlow Impeccable	Tumlow Odette	A. Collins	Mr. & Mrs. R. Harris

Name	Sex	Birth	Sire	Dam	Owner	Breeder
Tavey's Badge	F	14-4-70	Iceberg of Tavey	Nieta of Tavey	Mr. & Mrs. Somerfield	Mrs. J. Curnow
Studbriar Chieftain	M	12-8-68	Iceberg of Tavey	Eikon Jests Amazon	Mrs. M. King	Owner
Whistleberry Achilles	M	25-10-66	Clanguard Comanche	Clanguard Cha Cha	R. Wilson	H. Rooney
Yucca of Tavey	F	17-9-69	Iceberg of Tavey	Nieta of Tavey	Mrs. E. Edwards	Mrs. J. Curnow
Flexor Flugelman	M	24-3-70	Tumlow Green Highlander	Tumlow Radiance	D. Crick	Owner
Highroyds Avenger	M	29-7-71	Nayrilla Adonis	Queen Wilhelmina of Zonneleen	T. Lamb	Owner
Mitrasandra Gay Lady of Findjans	F	22-8-71	Tumlow Satan	Findjans Fair Allyne	Mr. & Mrs. Page	Mr. & Mrs. Taylor
Stroud of Reksum	M	4-5-68	Dante of Tramerfield	Candy of Tavey	Mrs. W. Barker	Mr. Musker
Tryphaena Titled Lady	F	14-7-71	Yachtsman of Tavey	Penny Poppet	Mrs. Harrington-Gill	C. Blackman
Tinkazan Serengetti	M	30-1-71	Tinkazan Triogen Texas Ranger	Tinkazan Serenissima	Mrs. J. Scheja	Owner
Tavey's Icypants	F	30-4-71	Iceberg of Tavey	Nieta of Tavey	Mrs. J. Curnow	Owner
Tavey's Gridiron	M	8-3-71	Yachtsman of Tavey	Rusa of Tavey	Mrs. J. Curnow	Owner
Vyleighs Valerian	F	3-2-72	Bonniedale Dougal	Hunsett Moonstone	R. Skinner	H. Vyse
Yachtsman of Tavey	M	17-9-69	Iceberg of Tavey	Nieta of Tavey	Mrs. J. Curnow	Owner
Heidi of Travemunde	F	16-6-71	Achim Zeitgeist	Jenifer of Travemunde	Mr & Mrs. A. Sheldon	Mr. J. Cole

Name	Sex	Date	Sire	Dam	Breeder	Owner
Achenburg Juliette	F	31–7–72	Triogen Tornado	Achenburg Delilah	Mr & Mrs. I. Wardropper	Mrs M. Woodward
Treasurequest Cristal	F	2–11–70	Treasurequest Annastock Xavier	Bronvorny's Black Glorious	Mr. & Mrs. R. Law	Mr. A. Brown
Tinkazan Shinimicas	F	11–1–73	Camerons Snoopy of Tinkazan	Triogen Timely Reminder	Mr. & Mrs. B. Hilliard	Mrs. J. Scheja
Heathermount Grenadier	M	29–3–71	Casper of Heathermount	Heathermount Quicksilver of Sonhende	Mrs. K. Kennaman	Mr. & Mrs. W. Parker
Tavey's Encore	F	14–5–74	Tavey's Satellite	Tavey's Icypants	Mrs. J. Curnow	Owner
Royaltains Miss Haversham	F	22–9–72	Triogen Tornado	Royaltains Snow Gem	Mr. G. Clark	Miss P. Quinn
Royaltains Highwayman of Borain	M	4–6–71	Royaltains Prince Regent	Royaltains Lunar Mirth	Mrs. P. Gledhill	Miss P. Quinn
Borain's Rageing Calm	F	20–3–74	Borain's Warning Shot	Borain's Born Forth	Mrs. P. Gledhill	Owner
Kenstaff Tornado of Achenburg	M	23–8–73	Triogen Tornado	Sundown Sheba	Mrs. M. Woodward	Mrs. I. Marshall
Kimvars Athos	M	10–3–71	Wilm Von Forell	Bankers Amethyst	Mr. H. Curtis	Owner
Demos Skipper	M	6–1–72	Tumlow Whiplash	Knotsalls Ezmaralda	Mr. M. Turner	Owner
Chevington Royal Black Magic	D	5.4.75	Hillmora the Extremist	Chevington Royal Chiffon	Mr. & Mrs. I. Ould	Mrs. O. Neave
Olderhill Seattle	B	4.2.74	Phileens Duty Free of Tavey	Olderhill Dhobi	Mrs. D. Patience	Mrs. S. Wilson

Name	Sex	Birth	Sire	Dam	Owner	Breeder
Dizown the Hustler	D	23.12.75	Tavey's Satellite	Olderhill Salvador	Mrs. D. Patience	Owner
Dizown Georgie Girl	B	23.12.75	Tavey's Satellite	Olderhill Salvador	Mr. & Mrs. J. James	Mrs. D. Patience
Olderhill Sheboygan	D	4.2.74	Phileens Duty Free of Tavey	Olderhill Dhobi	Mrs. S. Wilson	Owner
Findjans Poseidon	D	13.4.74	Phileens Duty Free of Tavey	Mitrasandra Gay Lady of Findjans	Mr. & Mrs. M. Page	Owner
Jatra's Raven	B	20.3.75	Findjans Poseidon	Jatra's Blue Star	Mr. B. Gazley	Owner
Royaltains Unexpected Guest	B	27.11.74	Royaltains Reluctant Hero	Mystic Gay Heroine	Miss P. Quinn	Mr. C. Brown
Copper Bronze Anoushka	B	26.6.74	Phileens Duty Free of Tavey	Sophie Copper Bronze	Mrs. S. Logan-Mitchell	Owner
Hillmora the Corsair	D	8.8.71	Wilm von Forell	Hillmora Triogen Torcella	Mrs. J. Baird	Mr. B. Johnson
Merrist Reluctant Knight	D	19.1.74	Royaltains Reluctant Hero	Tavey's Intrepid	Mrs. R. Scott	Mrs. G. Scott
Studbriar Dark N'Sassy of Zarwin	B	19.10.74	Studbriar Chieftain	Jatra's Commanche Princess	Mr. M. Jones	Mrs. M. King
Ariki Arataki	B	4.6.74	Studbriar Chieftain	Treasurequest Christal	Mrs. M. King	Mr. & Mrs. R. Law
Kaiserberg Helen	B	14.11.73	Kingsmeadow Blairderry Moss	Remberg's Bitter Sweet	Mr. D. More	Mrs. A. Buist
Arkturus Valans Choice	D	23.7.72	Linhoff the Pagan	Findjans Princess Pleasaunce	Mrs. V. Harle	Mr. J. Nolan

Lucinian Nera	D	18.6.71	Clanguard Comanche	Heidi of Garmondsway	Mr. R. Peters	Mr. P. Brooks
Abbeyville Shooting Star	B	24.4.73	Stroud of Reksum	Triogen Too True	Mr. R. Peters	Mr. W. Barker
Ainsdale Sea Marauder	D	31.1.71	Heidiland Trouble Spot	Annastock Waternymph	Mrs. J. Ainsley	Owner
Jasmere's Royal Melody	B	5.4.72	Tavey's Gentleman of Jasmere	Borains Born Free of Jasmere	Mrs. P. Judge	Mrs. J. Grove
Achenburg Juliette	B	31.7.72	Triogen Tornado	Achenburg Delilah	Mr. & Mrs. I. Wardropper	Mrs. M. Woodward
Upfolds Admiral Blackfoot	D	13.7.74	Yachtsman of Tavey	Lisa's Black and Tan Fantasy	Miss E. Bradley	Dr. Elliott
Hillmora the Explorer	D	8.12.73	Linhoff the Maestro	Hillmora the Capri	Mr. A. B. More	Mr. B. Johnson
Saxonhaus Black Bellman	D	9.5.71	Achim Zeitgeist	Saxonhaus Nayrilla Amethyst	Mrs. M. K. Stamps	Mrs. Hughes
Studbriar the Red	D	14.6.74	Phileens Duty Free of Tavey	Tavey's Renaissance	Mrs. M. King	Mrs. J. Curnow
Kaybar Rheingold	B	13.1.75	Greif von Hagenstern from Barrimilne	Karlakays Karmina	Mrs. A. Sturdy	Mr. & Mrs. K. Cole
Varla My Silk and Satin	B	1.3.73	Auldrigg Pinza	Zweite Madchen	Mr. & Mrs. S. Mackay	Mr. & Mrs. Valerio
Ashdobes Brown Berry	B	1.11.75	Cameron's Snoopy of Tinkazan	Ashdobes Venus	Mrs. S. Mitchell	Owner

Name	Sex	Birth	Sire	Dam	Owner	Breeder
Sandean Aquarius	D	24.2.74	Roanoke Goldfinger	Black Belinda	Mrs. R. Hedges	Mrs. T. Bruton
Ikos Valerians Valor	D	15.10.74	Triogen Tornado	Vyleighs Valerian	Mr. & Mrs. I. James	Mr. R. Skinner
Tavey's Ladyship of Shaheen	B	10.9.75	Tavey's Gridiron	Camereich Daytrip of Tavey	Mrs. E. Steggle	Mrs. J. Curnow
Chater Man of the Moment	D	16.8.72	Triogen Tornado	Baroness of Tavey	Mr. J. MacKenzie	Mrs. V. Killips
Davalog's Crusader	D	16.5.73	Tumlow Satan	Edwina Vivacious	Mr. & Mrs. A. Mullholland	Mr. F. Simmons
Javictreva Brief Defiance of Chater	D	6.4.75	Chater Icy Storm	Chater Moon Queen	Mrs. V. Killips	Mrs. N. Simmons
Borains Miss Royal	B	28.5.76	Flexor Flugelman	Borains Born Forth	Mrs. P. Gledhill	Owner
Major Marauder	M	18.12.76	Ainsdale Sea Marauder	Curdos Amarosa	Mr. & Mrs. T. Jones	Mrs. B. Horan
Alkay Alizanza	M	30.9.75	Stroud of Reksum	Roanoke Lucky Strike	Mr. W. Duggleby	A. Corbett
Dizown Bedazzled of Chaanrose	F	23.12.75	Tavey's Satellite	Olderhill Salvador	Mrs. R. Lane	Mrs. D. Patience
Phileens Ringmaster	M	13.8.74	Tavey's Satellite	Kay Hills Outrigger	Mrs. E. Edwards	Owner
Zalphas Harmony	F	10.10.75	Triogen Tornado	Jasmeres Royal Melody	Mrs. A. Richardson	Mrs. P. Judge
Studbriar the Godfather	M	3.10.76	Studbriar Chieftain	Jatra's Commanche Princess of Studbriar	Mr. A. Geraghty	Mrs. M. King
Pompie Alcyone	F	17.3.77	Findjans Poseidon	Pompie Sea Aphrodite	Mrs. H. Partridge	Owner

Auldrigg Witchcraft	F	6.9.71	Auldrigg Pinza	Auldrigg Pickety Witch	Mrs. F. Auld	Owner
Zalphas Spirit	F	22.12.77	Findjans Poseidon	Jasmeres Royal Melody	Mr. R. Moore	Mrs. P. Judge
Findjans Freya	F	8.3.77	Findjans Poseidon	Tanerdyce Michaelia	Mr. & Mrs. M. Page	Owners

OBEDIENCE CERTIFICATE WINNERS

OBEDIENCE CHAMPION (Winner of Three Obedience Certificates)

Name	Sex	Born	Sire	Dam	Breeder	Owner and Handler	Year of Win
Ch. Jupiter of Tavey	D	22–3–52	Bruno of Tavey	Prinses Anja v't Scheepjeskerk	Mrs. J. Curnow	Mrs. J. Curnow & Mr. R. M. Montgomery (Handler)	1954 & 1955

Winner of Two Obedience Certificates

Lionel of Rancliffe	D	13–8–63	Ch. Jove of Cartergate	Juliette of Rancliffe	Mrs. O. Morris	Mr. Derek Tretheway	1968

Winners of One Obedience Certificate

Yuba Adonis	D	18–5–60	Ch. & Ob.Ch. Jupiter of Tavey	Rotherhurst Celestial	Mrs. L. Hadley	Mr. Terry Hadley	1964
Heiner Rustic	D	26–2–62	Smoothfield Chico	Birchanger Dawn	Mr. Nash	Mr. Ian Inskip	1968

WORKING TRIALS WINNERS AND QUALIFIERS

WORKING TRIALS CHAMPIONS

Name	Sex	Born	Sire	Dam	Breeder	Owner	Handler	Stake won & Date
Ulf v. Margarethenhof, P.D.Ex., T.D.Ex., U.D.Ex., C.D.Ex.	D	30-6-64	Hasso v.d. Neckarstrasse	Toska v. Margarethenhof	Max Thurling	C.C. Surrey	Sgt. H. Darbyshire	P.D. 1949 P.D. 1950
Mountbrowne Karen, P.D.Ex., T.D.Ex., U.D.Ex.	B	18-8-50	Astor v. Morgensonne	Donathe v. Begertal	C.C. Surrey	C.C.Surrey	Pc. R. Ling	T.D. 1954 P.D. 1955
Mountbrowne Julie, P.D.Ex., T.D.Ex., U.D.Ex., C.D.Ex.	B	7-1-50	W.T.Ch. Ulf v. Margarethenhof	Donathe v. Begertal	C.C. Durham	C.C. Durham	Sgt. T. Sessford	T.D. 1955 P.D. 1955
Joseph of Aycliffe, P.D.Ex., T.D.Ex., U.D.Ex., C.D.Ex.	D	18-4-52	Dober v. Oldenfelde	W.T.Ch. Mountbrowne Julie	C.C. Durham	C.C. Durham	Sgt. W. McGorrigan	P.D. 1956 P.D. 1960

WINNERS OF ONE WORKING TRIALS CERTIFICATE

Name	Sex	Born	Sire	Dam	Breeder	Owner	Handler	Stake won & Date
Mountbrowne Joe, P.D.Ex., T.D.Ex., U.D.Ex., C.D.Ex.	D	7-1-50	W.T.Ch. Ulf v. Margarethenhof	Donathe v. Begertal	C.C. Surrey	Mary Porterfield (for Dobermann Club)	Owner	P.D. 1953
Mountbrowne Jenny, T.D.Ex., U.D.Ex.	B	7-1-50	W.T.Ch. Ulf v. Margarethenhof	Donathe v. Begertal	C.C. Surrey	C.C. Buckinghamshire	Sgt. G. Jones	T.D. 1952
Anna of Aycliffe, P.D.Ex., T.D.Ex., U.D.Ex., C.D.Ex.	B	16-4-55	W.T.Ch. Ulf v. Margarethenhof	Jenny of Aycliffen	C.C. Durham	C.C. Durham	Pc. Hutchinson	P.D. 1958
Arno of Aycliffe, P.D.Ex., T.D.Ex., U.D.Ex., C.D.Ex.	D	16-4-55	W.T.Ch. Ulf v. Margarethenhof	Jenny of Ayclifden	C.C. Durham	C.C. Durham	Sgt. H. Garth	P.D. 1959
Hawk of Trevellis, P.D.Ex., T.D.Ex., U.D.Ex., C.D.Ex.	D	10-6-62	Tavey's Stormy Legion	Brumbies Black Bramble	Mrs. D. Horton	Mr. H. Appleby	Owner	T.D. 1966

DOBERMANNS QUALIFYING AT CHAMPIONSHIP WORKING TRIALS

*Qualifying in Police Dog, Tracking Dog, Utility Dog & Companion Dog Stakes (P.D., T.D. U.D., C.D.)

Name	Sex	Born	Sire	Dam	Breeder	Owner	Handler
Vyking Drum Major	D	13–8–49	Vyking Don of Tavey	Vyking Wanda of Tavey	Mrs. P. Korda	Mrs. Jean Faulks	Owner
Mountbrowne Olaf	D	14–1–52	W.T.Ch. Ulf v. Margarethenhof	Donathe v. Begertal	C.C. Surrey	C.C. Surrey	Sgt. Taylor
Mountbrowne Amber	B	28–5–55	Mountbrowne Odin	Ch. Reichert Judy	Mrs. M. Porterfield	C.C. Northumberland	Pc. T. Yeopart, later Sgt. J. Hyslop

*Qualifying in Police Dog, Utility Dog & Companion Dog Stakes (P.D., U.D., C.D.)

Name	Sex	Born	Sire	Dam	Breeder	Owner	Handler
Mountbrowne Odin	D	14–1–52	W.T.Ch. Ulf v. Margarethenhof	Donathe v. Begertal	C.C. Surrey	C.C. Surrey	Pc. W. Redwood
Joan of Ayfelde	B	18–4–52	Dober v. Oldenfelde	W.T.Ch. Mountbrowne Julie	C.C. Durham	C.C. Durham	Pc. Hedges
Jenny of Ayclifden	B	18–4–52	Dober v. Oldenfelde	W.T.Ch. Mountbrowne Julie	C.C. Durham	C.C. Durham	Pc. Welsh
Faust of Cartergate	D	28–3–56	Ch. Day of Cartergate	Lola of Cartergate	Miss E. M. Would	C.C. Lincolnshire	Pc. J. Bush
Maverick the Brave	D	12–12–58	Ch. Challenger of Sonhende	Kaitonias Rio	Mr. C. Seddon	Mr. Colin Brockett	Owner
Yuba Adonis	D	18–5–60	Ch. & Ob.Ch. Jupiter of Tavey	Rotherhurst Celestial	Mrs. L. Hadley	Mr. Terry Hadley	Owner

*Qualifying in Tracking Dog, Utility Dog & Companion Dog Stakes (T.D., U.D., C.D.)

Name	Sex	Born	Sire	Dam	Breeder	Owner	Handler
Lorelei of Tavey	B	28–9–52	Tasso v.d. Eversburg of Tavey	Prinses Anja v't Scheepjeskerk	Mrs. J. Curnow	Mrs. Jean Faulks	Owner
Mountbrowne Remoh	D	26–5–53	Bill v. Blauen Blut	Mountbrowne Kandra	C.C. Surrey	C.C. Essex	Pc. P. Cousins
Mountbrowne Yukon	D	5–11–54	W.T.Ch. Ulf v. Margarethenhof	Ch. Reichert Judy	Mrs. M. Porterfield	C.C. Bedfordshire, later C.C. Surrey	Sgt. F. Pettit, later Pc. Proctor
Mountbrowne Astor	D	28–5–55	Mountbrowne Odin	Ch. Reichert Judy	Mrs. M. Porterfield	C.C. Devon	Pc. Kendrick
Barnard of Caedan	D	6–12–59	Culloden of Skipwith	Doberean Pamela	Mr. C. A. Beere	Mr. Ian Stewart	Owner
Gurnard Gloomy Sunday	D	1–11–63	Ch. Acclamation of Tavey	Gurnard Hedda	Mrs. D. Billingham & Mr. A. Barnard	Mrs. D. Billingham & Mr. A. Barnard	Mr. Alan Barnard

Qualifying in Tracking Dog, Working Dog, Utility Dog & Companion Dog Stakes (TD.; W.D., U.D., C.D.)

Name	Sex	Born	Sire	Dam	Breeder	Owner	Handler
Tavey's Stormy Jael	B	25-10-63	Ch. Tavey's Stormy Achievement	Tavey's Stormy Zeminda	Mrs. J. Curnow	Mrs. J. Curnow & Mrs. J. Faulks	Mrs. Jean Faulks
Dandy of Dovecote	D	6-2-63	Eddystone Lancelot	Smarty of Upend	Mr. M. Freeman	Mr. D. L. Milner	Owner
Dollar Premium	D	28-6-64	Ch. Turnlow Impeccable	Lacrosse Winning Ride	Mrs. E. Peckham	Mrs. Rosemary Hooper	Owner
Japonicas Ochre	D	26-8-67	Ch. Oberan of Tavey	Sal Pride of Edward	Mrs. Holt	Mr. & Mrs. Appleby	Mrs. Astrid Appleby
Chornytan Passenger	D	13-1-72	Tinsley's the Stormcloud	Chornytan Delight	Mrs. T. J. Toole	Mr. L. S. Christopher	Owner
Charis Aquarius	D	12-9-69	Trojan Achievement	Gretel Goddess of Gorsley	Mrs. A. Higgs	Mr. E. Handscomb	Owner
Koriston Pewter Strike of Doberean	B	22-7-72	Royaltains Nicky Tams	Doberean Eclat of Tavey	Mrs. A. E. Anderson	Mrs. Jean Faulks	Owner
Ch. Ashdobe's Brown Berry	B	1-11-75	Camerons Snoopy of Tinkazan	Ashdobe's Venus	Mrs. Sheila Mitchell	Mrs. Sheila Mitchell	Owner

*From 1969 to November 1979

Qualifying in Working Dog, Utility Dog & Companion Dog Stakes (W.D., U.D., D.C.)

Name	Sex	Born	Sire	Dam	Breeder	Owner	Handler
Wyndelhelm's Escort	D	4-4-67	Ch. Acclamation of Tavey	Ch. Wyndenhelm's AWOL	Mr. G. Thompson	Mr. George Thompson	Owner
Contessa of Achenburg	B	1-12-67	Xuberance of Tavey	Katina of Trevellis	Mrs. M. Woodward	Mr. Peter Leigh	Owner
Tumlow Solitaire	B	16-12-67	Apolda Blunderbuss	Tumlow the Witch	Mr. & Mrs. Harris	Mrs. Sheila Mitchell	Owner
Skipper of Ashdobe	D	27-11-69	Heiner Rustic	Tumlow Solitaire	Mrs. S. Mitchell	Mrs. Sheila Mitchell	Owner
Duchess Vanessa	B	22-10-70	Vanessa's Little Dictator of Tavey	Franskirby's Fireparade	Mr. Garrat	Mr. M. Thoulass	Owner
Jimarty's Macbeth of Vidal	D	30-7-71	Roanoke Double Diamond	Jimarty's Lancia Flavia	Mr. & Mrs. J. E. Burrell	Mr. C. Hooper	Owner
Danargo Dynamic	D	9-4-73	Ch. Triogen Tornado	Achenburg Fair Fortune	Mrs. A. L. Griffiths	Mr. A. L. Griffiths	Owner
Roanoke Serenade	B	2-12-75	Aust. Ch. Bonniedale Dougal	Black Baroness of Pintlehill	Mr. & Mrs. J. Richardson	Mr. & Mrs. A. Kingswell	Owner

Qualifying in Utility Dog Stakes (U.D.ex)

Name	Sex	Born	Sire	Dam	Breeder	Owner	Handler
Donathe v. Begertal	B	28-3-48	Zar v. Stahlhelm	Asta v. Teufenstal	Kurt Ehlebracht	C.C. Surrey	Sgt. A. Osment
Mountbrowne Justice	D	7-1-50	W.T.Ch. Ulf v. Margarethenhof	Donathe v. Begertal	C.C. Surrey	C.C. Kent	Sgt. S. Lawrie
Mountbrowne Juno	B	7-1-50	W.T.Ch. Ulf v. Margarethenhof	Donathe v. Begertal	C.C. Surrey	C.C. Lancashire	Sgt. H. Herdman
Mountbrowne Kim	D	18-8-50	Astor v. Morgensonne	Donathe v. Begertal	C.C. Surrey	C.C. West Riding	—
Brumbies Black Baroness	B	1-9-52	Carle of Combepeter	Betti of Cartergate	Mrs. P. Davis	Mr. David Kingsberry	Owner
Alouette of Aycliffe	B	16-4-55	W.T.Ch. Ulf. v. Margarethenhof	Jenny of Ayclifden	C.C. Durham	C.C. Durham	Pc. Aikenhead
Asta of Aycliffe	B	16-4-55	W.T Ch. Ulf. v. Margarethenhof	Jenny of Ayclifden	C.C. Durham	C.C. Durham	Pc. Brett
Diana of Aycliffe	B	11-8-57	Culloden of Skipwith	Joan of Ayfelde	C.C. Durham	C.C. Durham	—
Doberan Patience	B	30-3-59	Ch. Tavey's Stormy Abudance	Lorelei of Tavey	Mrs. J. Faulks	Mrs. Jean Faulks	Owner
Flame of Aycliffe	B	27-4-59	Culloden of Skipwith	Joan of Ayfelde	C.C. Durham	C.C. Bedfordshire	Pc. Fulcher
Fangio of Aycliffe	D	27-4-59	Culloden of Skipwith	Joan of Ayfelde	C.C. Durham	C.C. Dorset, later Mr. G. Clark	Pc. Williams, later Mr. R. Skelborne
Bracken of Cartergate	B	6-8-59	Ch. Claus of Cartergate	Ch. Helena of Cartergate	Miss E. M. Would	Mr. John Bush	Owner
Ch. Wyndenhelm's AWOL	B	25-7-60	Ch. Caliph of Trevellis	Ch. Bowesmoor Mona	Mr. G. Thompson	Mr. George Thompson	Owner
Goliath of Dissington	D	26-12-60	Bowesmoor Sancho	Bambi of Dissington	Mrs. E. M. Blair	C.C. Befordshire	Pc. N. Gorham
Wyndenhelm's Escort	D	4-4-67	Ch. Acclamation of Tavey	Ch. Wyndehlem's AWOL	Mr. G. Thompson	Mr. George Thompson	Owner
Lancon Skipper	D	31-7-51	Astor v. Morgensonne	Mountbrowne Juno	C.C. Lancashire	C.C. Lancashire	—
Mountbrowne Pluto	D	4-7-52	W.T.Ch. Ulf v. Margarethenhof	Mountbrowne Kandra	C.C. Surrey	C.C. East Riding	Pc. Peacock

Qualifying in Utility Dog Stakes (U.D. ex)

Name	Sex	Born	Sire	Dam	Breeder	Owner	Handler
Bowesmoor Gina	B	20-7-56	Treu v.d. Steinfurthohe	Helga v. Kleinwaldheim	Mrs. M. Porterfield	C.C. Essex	Pc. T. Bierne
Bowesmoor Herma	B	23-4-61	Old Boy	Vervain Rhythm	Mrs. M. Porterfield and Mr. H. Darbyshire	C.C. Devon	Pc. Farrow
Bowesmoor Otis	B	15-12-61	Smoothfield Chico	Doodloone Dear Delinquent	Mrs. D. H. Bamford	Mr. J. O. Whytock	Owner
Pagan Privateer	D	2-5-62	Ch. Acclamation of Tavey	Bracken of Cartergate	Mr. J. Bush	Mr. John Bush	Owner
Mountbrowne Peter	D	28-4-65	Fury of Dissington	Ina of Trevellis	Mr. M. V. Downes	C.C. Surrey	Pc. M. Juniper
Dena of Illustria	B	18-4-62	Illustria Tumlow Storm Ahead	Eurydice of Trevellis	Mrs. W. Garrod	Mr. M. J. Garrod	Owner
Harast Tomlyn	D	28-8-73	Japonicas Ochre	Hareaway Hebe	Mr. & Mrs. Appleby	Mr. & Mrs. Appleby	Mrs. Astrid Appleby
Helroy Hotspur	D	15-2-71	Chater Kings Reward	Helroy Lady Courage of Graybarry	Mrs. J. Glossop	Mr. L. Parker	Owner
Byron Burnt Sienna	B	21-4-75	Baron of Balbeggie	Swift of Balbeggie	Mrs. J. Stocks	Mr. P. J. Carrol	Owner

Qualifying 'U.D.'

Name	Sex	Born	Sire	Dam	Breeder	Owner	Handler
Astor v. Morgensonne	D	29-3-48	Sigmar	Asta v. Schulzenhof	Erich Raginski	C.C. Surrey	—
Prinses Anja v't Scheepjeskerk	B	3-7-48	Graaf Dagobert v. Neerlands Stam	Alindia v't Scheepjeskerk	Mrs. Kniiff Demout	Mrs. J. Curnow	Mrs. A. Montgomery
Mountbrowne Bruce	D	15-6-55	Alex v. Rodenaer	Mountbrowne Kandra	C.C. Surrey	C.C. Northumberland	Pc. Glendinning
Gin von Forell	D	23-1-60	Ger.Ch. Dirkv. Goldeberg	Diana vom Gelberg	Ernst Wilking	Mrs. M. Bastable	Owner

DOBERMANN CLUB WORKING TESTS DIPLOMA WINNERS (to November 1979)

Name	Sex	Born	Sire	Dam	Breeder	Owner & Handler	Test Passed
Lorelei of Tavey	B	28-9-52	Tasso v.d. Eversburg of Tavey	Prinses Anja v't Scheepjeskerk	Mrs. J. Curnow	Mrs. Jean Faulks	I II
Brumbies Bandit	D	8-3-55	Birtling Rebel	Brumbies Black Baroness	Mr. D. Kingsberry	Mr. D. Kingsberry	I
Carlo Eversburg of Romsley	D	2-4-58	Alex v. Rodenaer	Pride of Stonecross	Mr. J. C. Baugh	Mrs. Beryl Murphy	I
Triogen Tallulah	B	20-6-58	Ch. Tavey's Stormy Achievement	Triogen Bandeau of Tavey	Mr. A. B. Hogg	Mr. V. J. Lowe	I II
Mangrypin Sombrero	D	21-11-58	Treu v.d. Steinfurthohe	Mahadeo Early Edition	Mr. I. Bradbury	Mr. G. Myers	I
Maverick the Brave	D	12-12-58	Ch. Challenger of Sonheide	Kaitonia's Rio	Mr. C. Seddon	Mr. C. Brockett	I II III
Doberean Patience	B	30-3-59	Ch. Tavey's Stormy Abundance	Lorelei of Tavey	Mrs. J. Faulks	Mrs. Jean Faulks	I II
Ch. Wyndenhelms AWOL	B	25-7-60	Ch. Caliph of Trevellis	Ch. Bowesmoor Mona	Mr. G. Thompson	Mr. G. Thompson	I II IV
Dena of Illustria	B	18-4-62	Illustria Tumlow Storm Ahead	Eurydice of Trevellis	Mrs. W. Garrod	Mr. M. J. Garrod	I
Hawk of Trevellis	D	10-6-62	Tavey's Stormy Legion	Brumbies Black Bramble	Mrs. D. Horton	Mr. Bernard Horton later Mr. H. E. Appleby	I II III IV
Havildar of Trevellis	D	10-6-62	Tavey's Stormy Legion	Brumbies Black Bramble	Mrs. D. Horton	Mr. H. E. Appleby	I II III
Rhodesdobe Ousewhip Alethea	B	29-7-62	Mangrypin Sombrero	Smoothfield Diamond	Mr. G. Myers	Mr. K. Rhodes	I
Quizmaster of Siddley	D	19-1-63	Ch. Tavey's Stormy Wonder	November Mist of Siddley	Mr. V. J. Lowe	Mr. V. J. Lowe	I
Dandy of Dovecote	D	6-2-63	Eddystone Lancelot	Smarty of Upend	Mr. M. Freeman	Mr. D. L. Milner	I II III
Tavey's Stormy Jael	B	25-10-63	Ch. Tavey's Stormy Achievement	Tavey's Stormy Zeminda	Mrs. J. Curnow	Mrs. J. Curnow and Mrs. Jean Faulks (handler)	I II
Gurnard Gloomy Sunday	D	1-11-63	Ch. Acclamation of Tavey	Gurnard Hedda	Mrs. D. Billingham & Mr. A. Barnard	Mrs. D. Billingham & Mr. Alan Barnard (Handler)	I II III IV
Helroy Carrickgreen Climax	D	6-12-63	Carrickgreen Cordon Bleu	Carrickgreen Cluny	Mr. D. P. Clark	Mrs. J. Glossop	I
Fredo of Rhodesdobe	B	12-2-64	Ch. Annastock Lance	Rhodesdobe Ousewhip Alethea	Mr. K. Rhodes	Mr. K. Rhodes	I II

Name	Sex	Born	Sire	Dam	Breeder	Owner & Handler	Test Passed
Wyndenhelms Cormorant	B	8-6-64	Ch. Acclamation of Tavey	Ch. Wyndenhelms AWOL	Mr. G. Thompson	Mr. R. Hodge	I
Dollar Premium	D	28-6-64	Ch. Turnlow Impeccable	Lacrosse Winning Ride	Mr.s E. Peckham	Mrs. Rosemary Hooper	I II IV
Zonneleen Tammor Admiration	D	29-9-64	Ch. Tavey's Stormy Wonder	Rombermor Mein Chats	Mr. & Mrs. B. Roper	Mr. J. Wynne	I
Barrimilne Freshman	D	14-7-65	Gin von Forell	Brumbies Black Hornbeam	Mr. L. E. Wainwright	Mr. G. Kelly	I
Pompie the Bosun	D	12-7-64	Pompie Seaman	Hilton Rookery Flora Jane	Mr. A. J. Partridge	Mr. M. G. Page	I
Militiaman of Levenay	D	—	Ruptrech of Manford	Roma of Levenay	Mr. & Mrs. W. W. Berry	Mr. R. Cakebread	I
Gemsback of Deelcee	D	14-4-67	Ruptrech of Manford	Gazelle of Deelcee	Mr. D. E. Chandler	Mr. R. T. Gazley	I
Mountbrowne Peter	D	28-4-65	Fury of Dissington	Ina of Trevellis	Mr. M. V. Downes	C C Surrey (Handler Pc. M. Juniper)	I II
Eastern's Own	D	14-5-66	Vanessa's Little Dictator of Tavey	Devastation Top Girl	Mr. C. White	Mr. J. E. Burrell	I
Annastock Sirius	D	18-5-66	Ch. Tavey's Stormy Nugget	Annastock Kate of Sawgate	Mrs. J. Parkes	Mr. B. Pole	I
Hareaway Hamilton	B	5-7-66	Vanessa's Little Dictator of Tavey	Tavey's Stormy Beclette	Miss B. Elliott	Mr. C. Hooper	I II
Wyndenhelm's Escort	D	4-4-67	Ch. Acclamation of Tavey	Ch. Wyndenhelms AWOL	Mr. G. Thompson	Mr. George Thompson	I II
Chater Kings Reward	D	6-12-66	Ch. Crontham King	Heidiland High Society	Mrs. V. Killips	Mr. P. Eales	I
Helroy Lady Courage of Graybarry	B	1-4-66	Brumbies Barleycorn	Inga of Trevellis	Mr. E. W. Fletcher	Mrs. J. Glossop	I
Panzer of Kronsforde	D	17-2-64	Ch. Tavey's Stormy Master	Gerda of Kronsforde	Mr. H. Brookfield	Mr. H. Brookfield	I
Japonicas Ochre	D	26-8-67	Ch. Oberan of Tavey	Sal Pride of Edward	Mrs. Holt	Mr. H. E. Appleby	I II
Xerxes of Furzebeam	D	12-6-68	Edencourts Banker	Wyndenhelms Cormorant	Mr. R. Hodge	Mr. R. Hodge	I
Barrimilne Sheer Pride	B	27-2-68	Wilm von Forell	Barrimiline the Temptress	Mrs. M. Bastable	Mrs. C. Gudgeon	I
Gurnard Simon	D	20-9-67	Vanessa's Little Dictator of Tavey	Ch. Gurnard Gemma	Mrs. D. Billingham & Mr. A. Barnard	Mrs. D. Billingham & Mr. A. Barnard (handler)	I

Name	Sex	Born	Sire	Dam	Breeder	Owner & Handler	Test Passed
Pride of Cheshunt	B	15-7-68	Jammu Salmbukk	Katie's Biscuit Barrel	Mr. J. Pullan	Mr. L. Parker	I
Gin von Forell	D	23-5-60	Ger. Ch. Dirk v. Goldberg	Diana vom Gelberg	Herr Ernst Wilking	Mrs. M. Bastable	I
Turnlow Solitaire	B	16-12-67	Apolda Blunderbuss	Turnlow the Witch	Mr. & Mrs. R. Harris	Mrs. S. Mitchell	I II IV
Twilight Traveller	D	9-2-69	Dollar Premium	Heidi of Molsheim	Miss S. Elson	Miss S. Elson	I
Triogen Talent Spotter	D	26-9-68	Ch. Triogen Tornado	Triogen Tropical Splendour	Mr. A. B. Hogg	Mr. Griffiths	I
Charis Aquarius	D	12-9-69	Trojan Achievement	Gretel Goddess of Gorsley	Mrs. A. Higgs	Mr. E. Handscomb	I III III IV
Kudu of Furzebeam	B	3-2-65	Filibuster of Sonbende	Conquest of Dumbrill	Mrs. T. Puddephat	Mr. R. H. Jackson	I
Sym Comforter				No further details available		Mr. Moss	I
Skipper of Ashdobe	D	27-11-69	Heiner Rustic	Turnlow Solitaire	Mrs. S. Mitchell	Mrs. S. Mitchell	I II IV
Blitzkreiger of Eaton	D	23-5-68	Wilm von Forell	Jansue of Wyndham	Mr. D. Powell	Mr. Nosowitz	I
Placide of Tavey	B	5-6-68	Ch. Iceberg of Tavey	Rusa of Tavey	Mrs. J. Curnow	Mrs. J. Rutter	I
Oakfairs Debutante	B	9-10-68	Wilm von Forell	Oakfairs Carmen v. Riedlhof	Mr. and Mrs G. Turner	Mr. G. Turner	I
Hareaway Hebe	B	5-7-66	Vanessa's Little Dictator of Tavey	Tavey's Stormy Beclette	Miss B. Elliott	Mr. H. E. Appleby	I
Jimartys Lancia Flavia	B	9-2-69	Dollar Premium	Heidi of Molsheim	Miss S. Elson	Mrs. M. Burrell	I
Tavey's Alliance of Vidal	D	21-4-70	Kavkaunas Orbital Storm	Suffraget of Tavey	Mrs. J. Curnow	Mr. J. E. Burrell	I
Trumpkin Black Rose	B	2-7-70	Ch. Triogen Traffic Cop	Marnie from Ifieldwood	Mr. D. J. Evans	Mr. D. J. Evans	I II
Kickshaw of Furzebeam	B	20-3-66	Zouave of Furzebeam	Conquest of Dumbrill	Mrs. T. Puddephatt	Mrs. S. Gray	I
Achenburg Fair Fortune	B	3-11-70	Exclusive of Annastock	Baia of Achenburg	Mrs. M. Woodward	Mrs. A. L. Griffiths	I IA
Harast Astrid	B	31-7-71	Japonicas Ochre	Hareaway Hebe	Mr. & Mrs. Appleby	Mrs. L. Knapp	I
Helroy Hotspur	D	13-2-71	Chater Kings Reward	Helroy Lady Courage of Graybarry	Mrs. J. Glossop	Mr. L. Parker	I II III IV

Name	Sex	Born	Sire	Dam	Breeder	Owner & Handler	Test Passed
Chornytan Passenger	D	13-1-72	Tinsley the Stormcloud	Chornytan Delight	Mrs. T. J. Toole	Mr. L. S. Christopher	I II
Oakfairs Eulenspiegel	D	6-12-60	Timo v.d. Brunoburg	Oakfairs Carmen v. Riedlhof	Mr. & Mrs. G. Turner	Mr. G. Turner	I
Helroy Hot Cockles	B	13-2-71	Chater Kings Reward	Helroy Lady Courage pf Graybarry	Mrs. J. Glossop	Mr. P. Eales	I
Harast Joe	D	31-7-71	Japonicas Ochre	Hareaway Hebe	Mr. & Mrs. Appleby	Mrs. A. Warby	I
Pompie Sunset Shell	B	22-6-67	Easterns Own	Pompie Sea Urchin	Mrs. H. Partridge	Mr. M. Page	I
Karlakays Kruger	D	5-5-72	Wilm von Forell	Ch. Kingroy Karla Kay	Mr. Witham & Mr. O'Connor	Mr. E. Handscomb	I
Greenling Black Nugget	D	19-4-70	Lowenbrau Artisan of Courage	Tylerann Princess Starglow	Mrs. Linger	Mr. T. Fletcher	I
Helroy Hot Toddy	D	13-2-71	Chater Kings Reward	Helroy Lady Courage of Graybarry	Mrs. J. Glossop	Mr. J. Bushell	I
Helroy High Jump	D	2-6-68	Wilm von Forell	Helroy Lady Courage of Graybarry	Mrs. J. Glossop	Mr. R. Nosowitz	I
Darford Maxwell	D	22-7-69	Alex of Brandenberg	Lively Lady	Dr. A. Campbell	Mr. T. Radford	I
Illustria Elissa of Trevellis	B	9-11-59	Aguila of the Tamerlane	Classic of Trevellis	Mrs. D. Horton	Mr. M. J. Garrod	I
Duchess Vanessa	B	22-10-70	Vanessa's Little Dictator of Tavey	Frankskirbys Fireparade	Mr. Garrat	Mr. M. Thouless	I IA II III
Danargo Dynamic	D	9-4-73	Ch. Triogen Tornado	Achenburg Fair Fortune	Mrs. A. L. Griffiths	Mr. A. L. Griffiths	I IA II III IV
Illustria's Porthos	D	1-7-73	Xerxes of Furzebeam	Illustria's Eve	Mr. M. J. Garrod	Mr. M. J. Garrod	I
Rajah	D	16-2-72	Rajah	Emma	Not Known	Commissioner of the Metropolitan Police (Owner) Pc. R. Squire (Handler)	I II III
Great Tarquin	D	12-9-69	Trojan Achievement	Gretel Goddess of Gorsley	Mrs. A. Higgs	Mrs. Pamela Vaudrey	I II

Name	Sex	Born	Sire	Dam	Breeder	Owner & Handler	Test Passed
Koriston Pewter Strike of Doberean	B	22-7-72	Royaltains Nicky Tams	Doberean Eclat of Tavey	Mrs. A. E. Anderson	Mrs. Jean Faulks	I II
Ch. Ashdobe's Brown Berry	B	1-11-73	Cameron's Snoopy of Tinkazan	Ashdobe's Venus	Mrs. S. Mitchell	Mrs. Sheila Mitchell	I II
Ch. Hillmora the Explorer	D	8-12-73	Linhoff the Maestro	Hillmora the Capri	Mr. B. Johnson	Mr. A. B. More	I I A II
Gurnard Golla	D	8-7-74	Ch. Tumlow Satan	Demo's Soraya	Mr. A. Barnard	Mr. A. Barnard	I
Pompie Black Canasta	D	13-3-75	Ch. Arkturus Valans Choice	Pompie Sea Fleurette	Mr. A. J. Partridge	Mr. P. J. Carrol	I
Black's Sillhouette	B	1-5-73	Wilm von Forell	Finmear Black Pearl	Mr. D. L. Eaton	Mr. D. L. Eaton	I
Pompie Theseus	D	9-3-75	Ch. Arkturus Valans Choice	Pompie Sea Aquamarine	Mr. A. J. Partridge	Mr. B. K. Spiers	I
Quinsana Beau Gest of Ambari	D	26-8-74	Royaltains Olivers Twist	Royal Symbol of Chevington	Mrs. C. Smith	Dr. J. D. Patten	I
Woodlords Dominator	D	2-9-74	Tavey's Satellite	Rathkeel Penny Black	Mrs. C. J. Cowan	Mr. D. L. Eaton	I
Stonebank Happy Harry	D	10-10-74	Ch. Triogen Tornado	Hopemanne Happy Hilary	Mr. P. Williams	Mr. G. A. Bingham	I I A II
Kaiserbrg Bathtub Gin	B	21-12-74	Ch. Stroud of Reksum	Rembergs Bitter Sweet	Mrs. S. Buist	Mr. D. M. Coulter	I
Byron Burnt Sienna	B	21-4-75	Baron of Balbeggie	Swift of Balbeggie	Mr. J. Stocks	Mr. P. J. Carrol	I I A II
Ch. Chevington Royal Black Magic	D	5-4-75	Hillmora the Extremist	Chevington Royal Chiffon	Mrs. O. V. Neave	Mr. I. Ould	I I A II
Jovin-Blak Knite	D	24-11-73	Ch. Iceberg of Tavey	Eastern Feluccas	Mr. J. V. Alderson	Mr. J. V. Alderson	I I A
Jimartys Black Diamond Bay	D	13-8-76	Taveys Alliance of Vidal	Jimartys Sand Dancer	Mr. & Mrs. J. E. Burrell	Mr. J. Burrell	I I A
Tonio's Bombardier	D	6-6-76	Ch. Arkturus Valans Choice	Roving Moonspinner	Mr. R. Peacock	Mr. M. Thouless	I I A
Findjans Ikeya-Seki	D	26-4-75	Phileens Duty Free of Tavey	Ch. Mitrasandra Gay Lady of Findjans	Mr. & Mrs. M. G. Page	Mr. H. Whiter	I I A
Schneider of Mercia	D			No Further Particulars		Mr. P. Lakin	I
Garath St. David	D	Dec. 1974		"Rescue" Dog, so breeding unknown		Mr. J. Middleweek	I I A
Black Ice	D	21-5-76	Philleens Duty Free of Tavey	Helaman Beatrice	Mrs. A. Y. Higgs	Mrs. Iris Green	I I A II
Jovin Blak Jeny	B	24-11-73	Ch. Iceberg of Tavey	Eastern Feluccas	Mr. J. V. Alderson	Mr. Ward	I
Vyleighs Mustang	D	28-6-76	Canterilla Cutlass	Vyleighs Strider	Mrs. H. M. Vyse	Mrs. H. M. Vyse	I

Parabar Black Chiffon	B	7-4-77	Ch. Chevington Royal Black Magic	Tavey's Lamé	Mrs. B. Grant-Parkes	Mrs. Mary Ould	I
Charcoal Lady	B	26-3-77	Tinsleys March from Sousa	Bronze Venus	Mrs. N. O. Poulton	Mr. K. Rhodes	I IA
Sandjar of Jimartys	D	13-5-77	Taveys Satellite	Jimartys Flexabella	Mr. & Mrs. J. E. Burrell	Mr. J. Burrell	I
Luke the Drifter	D	31-8-76	Chaka the Warrior	Demo the Adventuress	Mrs. S. Fitchett	Mr. S. Dawes	I
Jimartys Sandlmans	D	22-6-76	Jimartys Sandman	Jimartys Cressida	Mr. & Mrs. J. E. Burrell	Mrs. P. Ainsworth	I
Chater French Connection	D	24-4-76	Ch. Javictreva Brief Defiance of Chater	Chater High Society	Mrs. V. J. Killips	Mr. K. D. Clarke	I
Thelos Orea Gobelaz	B	19-9-77	Sea King	Pompie Sea Fenella	Mr. & Mrs. B. R. Bennett	Mr. D. Dennis	I
Frankskirby Jubilee Flame	D	5-6-77	Phileens American Express	Frankskirby Red Christel	Mr. & Mrs. B. M. J. Spaughton	Mrs. C. Tucker	I
Roanoke Serenade	B	2-12-75	Aust. Ch. Bonniedale Dougal	Black Baroness of Pintlehill	Mr. & Mrs. J. Richardson	Mr. A. Kingswell	I
Jubilee Queen of Jimartys	B	13-5-77	Taveys Satellite	Jimartys Flexabella	Mr. & Mrs. J. E. Burrell	Mr. E. Handsford	I
Koriston Polonaise of Dobetran	B	5-4-78	Royaltains Nicky Tams	Koriston Superstarlet	Mrs. A. E. Anderson	Mrs. Jean Faulks	I

APPENDIX I

DOBERMANNS IN POLICE SERVICE

Name	Sex	Born	Sire	Dam	Breeder	Owner	Handler
Ulf v. Margarethenhof	D	30-6-46	Hasso v.d. Neckarstrasse	Toska v. Margarethenhof	Max Thurling	C.C. Surrey	Sgt. H. Darbyshire
Astor v. Morgensonne	D	29-3-48	Sigmar	Asta v. Schulzenhof	Erich Raginski	C.C. Surrey	—
Donathe v. Begertal	B	28-3-48	Zar v. Stahlhelm	Asta v. Teufenstal	Kurt Ehlebracht	C.C. Surrey	Sgt. A. Osment
Mountbrowne Joe / Justice / Juno / Jenny / Julie	D / D / B / B / B	7-1-50	W.T.Ch. Ulf v. Margarethenhof	Donathe v. Begertal	C.C. Surrey	Mrs. M. Porterfield for the Dobermann Club / C.C. Kent / C.C. Lancashire / C.C. Buckinghamshire / C.C. Durham	Mrs. Mary Porterfield / Sgt. S. Lawrie / Sgt. H. Herdman / Sgt. G. Jones / Sgt. T. Sessford
Mountbrowne Karen / Kandra / Kola / King / Kim	B / B / B / D / D	18-8-50	Astor v. Morgensonne	Donathe v. Begertal	C.C. Surrey	C.C. Surrey / C.C. Surrey / C.C. West Riding / C.C. Suffolk / C.C. West Riding	Pc. Ling / — / — / — / —
Mountbrowne Odin / Olaf / Onyx / Otis	D / D / D / B	14-1-52	W.T.Ch. Ulf v. Margarethenhof	Donathe v. Begertal	C.C. Surrey	C.C. Surrey / C.C. Cheshire / C.C. East Sussex / C.C. Cheshire	Pc. W. Redwood / Sgt. Taylor / Pc. Horscroft / —
Mountbrowne Pablo / Pluto / Pedro / Pinto / Paula	D / D / D / D / B	4-7-52	W.T.Ch. Ulf v. Margarethenhof	Mountbrowne Kandra	C.C. Surrey	C.C. Cheshire / C.C. East Riding / — / C.C. Dorset	Pc. Peacock / — / — / —
Mountbrowne Remoh / Reina	D / B	26-1-53	Bill v. Blauen Blut	Mountbrowne Kandra	C.C. Surrey	C.C. Essex / C.C. Kent, later / C.C. Surrey	Pc. P. Cousins / —
Mountbrowne Tasco / Tasso / Taxel	D / D / D	24-3-54	W.T.Ch. Ulf v. Margarethenhof	Mountbrowne Kandra	C.C. Surrey	C.C. Hertfordshire / C.C. Lancashire / C.C. Shropshire	Pc. E. Pugh / Pc. Alston / Pc. Roberts
Mountbrowne Yukon / Yager	D / D	5-11-54	W.T.Ch. Ulf v. Margarethenhof	Ch. Reichert Judy	Mrs. M. Porterfield	C.C. Bedfordshire, later C.C. Surrey	Sgt. F. Pettit, later Pc. Proctor

Name	Sex	Born	Sire	Dam	Breeder	Owner	Handler
Mountbrowne Amber	B	28-5-55	Mountbrowne Odin	Ch. Reichert Judy	Mrs. M. Porterfield	C.C. Northumberland	Pc. T. Yeouart, later Sgt. J. Hyslop
Astor	D					C.C. Devon	Pc. Kendrick
Arras	D						—
Alger	D						
Mountbrowne Barry	D	15-6-55	Alex v. Rodenaer	Mountbrowne Kandra	C.C. Surrey	C.C. Kent	Pc. Glendinning
Bruce	D					C.C. Northumberland	—
Mountbrowne Dinco	D	20-11-55	W.T.Ch. Ulf v. Margarethenhof	Mountbrowne Reina	C.C.Surrey	C.C. Surrey	Pc. W. Redwood
Mountbrowne Shifta	D		Further	particulars	unknown	C.C. Surrey	—
Mountbrowne Peter	D	28-4-65	Fury of Dissington	Ina of Trevellis	Mr. M. V. Downes	C.C. Surrey	Pc. M. Juniper
Copper of Buckinghamshire	D	31-7-51	Astor v. Morgensonne	Mountbrowne Juno	C.C. Lancashire	C.C. Buckinghamshire	—
Lancon Skipper	D					C.C. Lancashire	—
Lancon Pilot	D					C.C. Lancashire	Pc. Rolands
Joan of Ayfelde	B	18-4-52	Dober v. Oldenfelde	W.T.Ch. Mountbrowne Julie	C.C. Durham	C.C. Durham	Pc. P. Hedges
Jenny of Ayclifden	B						Pc. Welsh
Joseph of Aycliffe	D						Pc. W. McGorrigan
Arno of Aycliffe	D	16-4-55	W.T.Ch. Ulf v. Margarethenhof	Jenny of Ayclifden	C.C. Durham	C.C. Durham	Pc. H. Garth
Argus	D						Pc. S. Regan
Anna	B						Pc. Hutchinson
Asta	B						Pc. Brett
Alouette	B						Pc. Aikenhead
Adella	B						Pc. Scott
Amanda	B						—
Anita	B						Pc. Wheatley
Diana of Aycliffe	B	11-8-57	Culloden of Skipwith	Joan of Ayfelde	C.C. Durham	C.C. Durham	—
Flame of Aycliffe	B	27-4-59	Culloden of Skipwith	Jenny of Ayclifden	C.C. Durham	C.C. Bedfordshire	Pc. Fulcher
Fangio	D					C.C. Dorset, later Mr. W. G. Clark	Pc. Williams, later Mr. R. Skelhorne
Argus of Northumbia	D	29-5-59	Bowesmoor Kuno	Mountbrowne Amber	C.C. Northumberland	C.C. Northumberland	Pc. Crisp
John v. Waldhorst	D	22-6-60	Lasso v. Zyraksgarten	Quinda v.d. Ansbornquelle	—	C.C. Durham	Pc. S. Regan
Greif	D	7-4-55	Bruno of Tavey	Baba Black Sheep	Mrs. D. M. Ince	C.C. Hertfordshire	Pc. H. Appleby
Faust of Cartergate	D	28-3-56	Ch. Day of Cartergate	Lola of Cartergate	Miss E. M. Would	C.C. Lincolnshire	Pc. J. Bush
Goliath of Dissington	D	26-12-60	Bowesmoor Sancho	Bambi of Dissington	Mrs. E. M. Blair	C.C. Bedfordshire	Pc. N. Gorham

Name	Sex	Born	Sire	Dam	Breeder	Owner	Handler
Fagin	D	7-8-65	Zouave of Furzebeam	Highbrooks Andromeda	Mr. M. Witham	C.C. Hertfordshire	Pc. E. Pugh
Bowesmoor Dana	B	26-5-73	Bill v. Blauen Blut	Mountbrowne Kandra	C.C. Surrey	C.C. Dorset	Pc. P. Thrasher, later Sgts Highmore & Green
Bowesmoor Gina	B	20-7-76	Treu v.d. Steinfurthöhe	Helga v. Kleinwaldheim	Mrs. M. Porterfield	C.C. Essex, later C.C. Hertfordshire	Pc. T. Bierne
Bowesmoor Herma Hain Hero	B D D	23-4-61	Old Boy	Vervain Rhythm	Mrs. M. Porterfield & Mr. H. Darbyshire	C.C. Devon C.C. Devon Commissioner of the Metropolitan Police	Pc. Farrow Pc. Lane Pc. Geeves
Metpol Fritz	D	Prob.1955	Birling Roimond	Frieda von Casa Mia of Upend	Mr. L. Hamilton Renwick	Commissioner of the Metropolitan Police	Pc. Dines
Rajah	D	16-2-72	Rajah	Emma	Not Known	Commissioner of the Metropolitan Police	Pc R. Squire

BIBLIOGRAPHY

CURNOW, FRED. *The Dobermann* (booklet), n.d.

GRUENIG, PHILIPP. *The Dobermann Pinscher*, Orange Judd, New York, 1951.

NOTED BREED AUTHORITIES. *The Complete Dobermann Pinscher*, Howell Book House, New York, 1967.

SCHMIDT, WILLIAM *The Dobermann Pinscher*, Judy Publishing Co., Chicago, 1935.

SPIRER, LOUISE ZIEGLER AND MILLER, EVELYN. *This Is The Dobermann Pinscher*, T.F.H. Publications, New Jersey, 1963.

INDEX